LifeOvers

LifeOvers

Upside-Down
Ways to Become More
Like Jesus

GRACIE MALONE

Revell
Grand Rapids, Michigan

Published by Fleming H. Revell
a division of Baker Publishing Group
P.O. Box 6287, Grand Rapids, MI 49516-6287

Printed in the United States of America

ISBN 978-0-7394-8182-0

Published in association with the literary agency of Alive Communications, Inc., 7680 Goddard Street, Suite 200, Colorado Springs, CO 80920.

To Dr. John Morris, our pastor, friend, counselor, and advisor on things theological. Thank you for your ministry to the Malone clan—to Joe and me, to our children, and to our children's children. I couldn't have written this book without your inspiration and help. May God bless you richly.

Contents

Not until we have become humble and teachable,
standing in awe of God's holiness and sovereignty . . .
acknowledging our own littleness,
distrusting our own thoughts,
and willing to have our minds turned upside down,
can divine wisdom become ours.

J. I. Packer

Foreword

When Gracie Malone first asked me to write the foreword for this book, I immediately said yes—not because I had read the content, but because I believe in Gracie. She's one of those rare, wise women who has lived long enough to combine biblical truth with the reality of living in a fallen world. What comes out of her mouth and from her pen (okay, from her computer) is the ideal mixture of common sense and an understanding of tough issues that she sifts through the grid of the Word of God—and suddenly you say, "I *get* it! This concept I've been trying to understand makes sense now." Add to that Gracie's ability to weave stories throughout her teaching with just the right combination of laugh-out-loud humor and fresh-from-life narrative, and you have a book you can't put down.

The manuscript arrived, and I gulped as I was reminded of the theme: *LifeOvers: Upside-Down Ways to Become More Like Jesus*. Gracie knew I had been living upside down since the arrest of my son for first-degree murder. My only child, a graduate of the U.S. Naval Academy with an impeccable record, had been convicted of first-degree murder and sentenced to life without the possibility of parole in the state of Florida. Yes, my life has been very upside-down from the life I thought I would be living at this point in my journey. I anticipated having my son and his wife and their precious children around my Christmas tree and my Thanksgiving table. I envisioned a happy, glorious future for our little family—but that is *not* my story. My husband and I spend our at-home Saturdays and Sundays in a maximum security prison visiting our son, who, humanly speaking, has a hopeless future. But God . . .

This book is about the "But God" factor in life. Gracie skillfully teaches us how to get a grip on life no matter what our expectations, misinterpretations, and long-ingrained false concepts have been about specific Scriptures and biblical principles. Those of you who know Gracie only as a humorist, a grandparenting specialist, or an entertaining and engaging speaker may be surprised at the profound scriptural depth in this book. While giving up none of her sense of humor and practical applications, she skillfully teaches us how to embrace the Christlike life—or *ChristLife*, as Gracie calls it—even when what's happening around us doesn't make sense.

Gracie's gift to each reader is that her content will cause you to think, to question the way you've always interpreted a certain biblical concept, and to dig deeper into God's Word to find out if your understanding of that principle is founded on a firm foundation or on a faulty one. Don't read this book if you are content with your spiritual life the way it is. *LifeOvers* is a book for women who are ready for the adventure of a lifetime! If you want to begin encouraging other women to become more Christlike, and if you want to understand the treasures in the Bible, dig in—and don't be surprised when God starts using *you* to impact others to become women of influence for his glory.

Even though my life has turned out differently than the one I had envisioned on my personal goal chart, understanding the upside-down truth—that there's spiritual strength in weakness—renews my faith. Gracie reminds all of us that life comes out of death and redemption can come out of situations that seem hopeless. This book reveals the secret strength that is yours to experience when you embrace (not endure) the reality of the ChristLife.

Gracie Malone is my friend—but she is also my teacher. Thanks, Gracie, for leading me to a new way of living through this extraordinary book!

Carol Kent,
international speaker;
author, *When I Lay My Isaac Down* (NavPress)

I challenge you to read through the chapter titles of this book and pick the first "upside-down truth" that pricks a nerve in your belief system. Start there. This book is ideal for personal study or for small group interaction. Begin by going through it on your own, and then gather a group of women together for a twelve-week study that will lead them to personal transformation. You will discover the discussion questions in the Right-Side Up section at the end of each chapter will demand honesty, authenticity, and a study of biblical truth that will produce positive change.

Be sure to invite women from varying age groups and different levels of spiritual maturity. Commit to each other that what is discussed during the study of this book will go no further. Pray together at the end of each session. This book will undoubtedly produce friendships for a lifetime, along with the kind of accountability that develops spiritual maturity.

Carol Kent

1

A New Way of Living

Embracing the ChristLife

Now this is eternal life: that they may know you, the only true God, and Jesus Christ, whom you have sent.

John 17:3

On December 26, 2004, a great earthquake measuring a whopping 9.5 on the Richter scale struck in the Indian Ocean. The earthquake was so powerful it caused our planet to tilt on its axis. According to scientists, time will forever be altered by a quarter of one second, and the map of Asia will need to be redrawn.

The quake also caused a tidal wave, a tsunami, that swept away vacationers and residents of Sri Lanka, Indonesia, Thailand, Malaysia, the coast of India, and other places. More than a dozen countries were devastated by the churning water of twenty- to thirty-foot waves. The final death toll eventually reached a staggering 215,000. It was a tragedy of apocalyptic proportions.

While the tsunami took its victims completely by surprise, we can be sure that our all-knowing God was not caught off guard. In fact, more than two thousand years ago, Jesus warned his followers to expect tsunami-like calamities during "the last days." Listen to his prophetic words: "Upon the earth dismay among nations, in perplexity at the roaring of the sea and the waves" (Luke 21:25 NASB).

As I watched the catastrophic scene replayed again and again on TV, my heart went out to those whose lives had been so quickly, radically changed. The faces portrayed on the screen in my living room revealed the deep-seated pain the men, women, and children were feeling—broken hearts over the loss of a loved one, confusion about what had happened, fear about what might happen next, "perplexity at the roaring of the sea and the waves."

Eventually, my thoughts shifted from this decimating tragedy to another type of tidal wave, one that threatens to swamp families every day. Aftershocks that come when children make wrong choices. The jagged fissures of divorce. Floods of disappointment that wash away hope. This kind of tragedy has a face also—faces that reflect the same confusion and fear.

Thankfully, in times like these, we find words of comfort in the Bible: "Let not your heart be troubled." "I have loved you with an everlasting love." These and other promises are scattered throughout its pages like sparkling jewels, easily spotted, there for the taking. But other treasures lie buried deep in the sea of God's Word, pearls of wisdom tucked inside a tightly closed shell. These are a bit harder to find. (Think deep-sea diving versus a walk on the beach.) But

opening them up is worth the effort—a find that's unfor-
gettable, life changing.

In my personal Bible study, I've discovered some "pearls"
that I call "Upside-Down Truths." They are those two-sided
teachings, concepts that cause me to scratch my head and
require me to dig deep to figure out what they really mean.
To me they seem upside down, because at first glance they
appear one way but upon further study reveal something
exactly opposite. They present the dichotomies of our spiritual life.

We experience pain and, in the midst of it, find joy. We
suffer and, at the same time, rejoice. We discover strength
in weakness, find peace in the midst of trouble, and in our
darkest moments, see brilliant light. As we mature we don't
become more adult, more grown-up, but more childlike,
and in the process discover that, even though flawed and
broken, we are deeply and unconditionally loved. As we
struggle to let go of certain issues or try to stop controlling other people, we feel as if we might literally die, but
amazingly we find life.

These are only a few of the upside-down concepts I've
explored in this book. The Bible is full of such teachings,
but these are enough to provide you with a firm foundation
when personal storms threaten. Your faith, your ability to
lean into these truths, like steering your craft into the wind,
enables you to navigate the troubled waters and sail into
a quiet harbor where you may be safe.

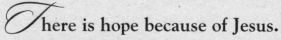

here is hope because of Jesus.
Bob E. Hamilton

My friend Carolyn navigated many a turbulent sea before
she found refuge in God. Let me introduce her.

She and I have been friends for more years than either of us care to admit (okay, at least twenty-five!). We've celebrated with each other at baby showers, baptisms, graduations, weddings, and a funeral or two. And, being mothers of sons (her two and my three), we've also survived Little League, soccer games, driver's education, high school football, confusing awards ceremonies, and more than a few rather sobering parent-teacher conferences. In recent years Carolyn laughs with me over the funny things my grandkids say, and I listen when she talks about her new daughter-in-law and deals with her empty nest.

It's interesting to me how friendships develop and how unique each friend-to-friend relationship is. Since I'm at least ten years older than Carolyn, some might wonder how we ever got connected at all. Maybe it was her all-American-girl manner or her bright smile that made me want to be her friend. Or maybe it was her thoughtful disposition, the way she asked questions, the way she listened when I talked. At any rate, the first time she showed up at my Bible study group, I suggested we meet for coffee and get better acquainted. Thus began a friendship that has not only lasted but has been one of my greatest blessings.

Carolyn is my deep-thinking friend, the one I call when I'm puzzling over the meaning of a certain Greek word or when I'm thinking about how to untangle some complicated relationship problem. She's a student of God's Word, a devoted teacher, and a mentor to younger women. To say that she loves the Lord would be an understatement. He is her life (Col. 3:4). Recently Carolyn said, "You know, the Christian life is not really about our trying to be *like* Jesus, which requires a lot of self-effort. It's just Jesus. Period."

Of course I agree. And even though the thought of it may seem a bit upside down to our usual way of thinking, perhaps we all should stop trying to imitate Jesus and simply relax in fellowship with him. To me that's the *ChristLife*: him abiding in our hearts, doing his work from the inside out, rather than us working from the outside in.

Carolyn tells us how she arrived at this place in her journey:

I am the oldest of four children with a younger sister and two brothers. We grew up on a farm in West Texas where there was always work to be done. My sister and I did lots of housework, and my brothers worked on the farm with our dad. It was during those days that I first began to realize I was not like other kids my age. Maybe it was an inborn personality trait or just being a bit dysfunctional. But no matter the reason why, the truth is I can't remember a time when I didn't feel a big empty spot in my heart. Seems I was always looking for approval and love—more than what my mother and daddy could give me.

I began to feel better when at the tender age of nine, I asked Jesus to be my Lord. It happened one evening after a revival service. I had been troubled by the pastor's sermon and afterward asked my dad several questions about salvation. He called our pastor, who came over to our house and explained that Jesus had died for my sins, that he wanted me to believe the truth and receive him into my heart (see John 1:12). As I sat on my daddy's lap, I prayed, asking Jesus to forgive me of my sins and to change my life. I became a Christian that night, but looking back on my life now, I actually knew very little about embracing what I had believed.

For one thing, I didn't know how to handle my emotions, especially my anger. Because I never learned to express it, my feelings turned inward and I became depressed. As I grew from a young girl into a teenager, I couldn't figure out why I felt so bad. It definitely wasn't rational. I had everything—a nice home, good parents, security, friends. Besides that, I excelled at sports. Still, my feelings didn't line up. I remember people saying, "You shouldn't feel so bad, look at what you have. Count your blessings." Even though I know they meant well and were trying to help, their comments only caused me more pain—guilt on top of depression.

After high school and into college, I continued to feel bad. The hole was still there in my heart, and I became desperate to fill it. Unfortunately, I sought to fill the void in ways that did not please God. Thus began a destructive cycle—deep depression, temporary relief, unresolved guilt, then even deeper depression. This pattern persisted into young adulthood.

I was trying to hold down a job while living far away from home and struggling with relationship problems. I became so depressed that I could barely function. When I wasn't working, I would sink to the floor of my apartment, where I would sit for hours and hours. I couldn't move from my spot on the floor except to go to the bathroom. At other times, I was so emotionally exhausted that I'd sleep sixteen to eighteen hours, be up six, then do it again. Finally I saw a psychiatrist.

Four times a week I'd set my alarm for five a.m., pull on some clothes, and drive more than an hour to the doctor's office. After my appointment, I'd somehow make it to work, then I'd head back home to my spot on the floor. The doctor treated me for several months. He didn't prescribe any medication, but helped me learn some important coping skills. Of course, I know now there can be no real healing unless it is spiritual healing, unless God does it.

At any rate, I got well enough to land the job of my dreams. I moved to California and became an international flight attendant. The excitement of being able to travel to foreign countries provided a temporary emotional lift. At times, I still struggled with depression, but at least I was functioning and even having fun. During this time I met Jim, my future husband, the father of our two sons. Jim became a Christian during the four years we dated. After we married we lived three years in Minnesota before moving to Texas.

As we settled into our new surroundings in the state where I'd grown up, you'd think I'd be happy. But the old feelings of depression came back. None of it made sense. I had a good life—a great husband with a good job, two precious little boys, and material things. But life was tough for me. It may sound confusing, but I know that a person can have all the stuff of life and still feel that life isn't worth living. It was during this frustrating time that we joined a church and met its pastor. It was also the time I met Gracie. It was from her I learned that our pastor did biblical counseling and it was free! One day I called the church office and made an appointment with him.

During my first visit with him, he said something I will never forget. Looking into my tear-streaked face, he declared confidently, "There is hope because of Jesus." Throughout the next few months as I met with him regularly, that promise became a sort of lifesaver for me. Even when I didn't feel like hoping, I hung onto those words. Eventually they proved to be amazingly true.

Pastor Hamilton was not only a good counselor but he was an avid disciple maker. The first thing he did was assign some homework—a series of Bible study booklets for me to work through. As I completed step one, then two, and eventually step ten, I was accountable to him. He checked my work, and we'd talk about my answers. He also gave me dozens of good books to read. None of them were primers. I read mind-stretching books like *Knowing God* by J. I. Packer, *Holiness* by J. C. Ryle, and William Gurnall's *The Christian in Complete Armor*. I read books about self-image, including *You Are Very Special* by Verna Birkey. I attended several Bible study classes. Through this process, I was discovering that the Bible really did have the answers to life's struggles, and I was growing in both knowledge and grace (2 Peter 3:18).

Occasionally, during our weekly meetings, my pastor would encourage me to open up about the personal matters that were troubling me. For months I would say, "I'm not ready." He was kind and patient, answering, "Someday you may need to tell me." Then one day he gave me a book about sin. I don't remember the title, but its message broke my heart into a million pieces. For the first time in my life I saw that my sin had nailed Jesus to the cross. I wept and wept and wept because of my sin. At our next appointment, I began vomiting out details about my past. It took most of the morning. When I walked out of his office, I was so deeply troubled that he thought I shouldn't be alone. He asked one of the church's secretaries to go home with me. She sat with me all afternoon. The next morning I went back to his office and vomited out more. The next day there was more. When all of that was out, there was a rushing in of peace and forgiveness and freedom. It was life changing. That day, the dark cloud lifted, and it has not settled over me again.

Nobody but God can do that. It took a moving of his grace. It was God's grace that brought me to a place of despair so the hole in my life could be filled with himself. It took grace for me to see it, grace to say it, grace to receive it, and it takes grace to live it day by day.

Today, I have absolute security. God has given me peace that literally passes all human understanding, and I have great joy—not a giddy, slap-happy feeling that may come and go, but the kind of joy that abides no matter what the circumstances. That doesn't mean that my life is pain free. There are still things that have to be forgiven, sins that are revealed, periods of dryness, problems dealing with pride and shame. And there are times when I feel blue. God didn't change my personality. But I'm determined to wait on him.

He's the only way anything can be fixed. If some things in this life are never solved, some wounds are never healed, my times are in his hands. And I know that someday in heaven that hole will be completely filled. That's how I live my life.

Can you relate to Carolyn's story? Do you know that kind of peace? That kind of joy? Or perhaps you can't relate to the feelings of my friend. Maybe you have never felt a depressed day. Whether you live in eternal sunshine emotionally or fight off dark clouds, you still need Jesus.

You **have made us for yourself, O God, and our hearts are restless until they find their rest in you.**

Augustine

When the Asian tsunami hit, there were several isolated tribes living on India's Andaman and Nicobar islands, in the very vortex of the storm. Through the years, environmentalists had closely watched these small groups while protecting the tribes' freedom to live life their own way, much as their ancestors had lived thousands of years ago. Scientists feared that because of their fragile tribal societies, they might be completely wiped out, thus losing an important piece of history and an important link in the chain of human development.

As soon as the waters receded, helicopters circled over the islands searching for any sign of life. When the islanders heard the helicopters' propellers pounding the air over their villages, they ran out of their hiding places and shot a volley of arrows in their direction. This not only startled but delighted the pilots. As amazing as it may seem, not a single tribe member was lost. Apparently they survived because of their close connection to nature. Ajoy Bagchi, an Indian environmentalist, explained, "They still retain the ancient wisdom. They could read the signs of nature. They read the signs and disappeared deep into the jungle where they were completely safe."[1]

How interesting!

Do you think it possible for women like you and me to be so connected to God, so full of his wisdom, that the storms of life will not catch us off guard? I am counting on it!

So even though I'm not ready to give up my Palm Pilot, my iPod, or my cellular phone, neither will I let go of the "ancient wisdom" that keeps me grounded.

When everything we've considered rock solid is swept away, when the terra firma liquefies beneath our feet, there is one Rock that remains. Unmovable! Unchangeable! And that Rock is Christ. May we lock arms with him as we begin living "Upside Down."

$\mathcal{R}$ight-Side Up

1. Read Psalm 27:1–5. Apparently the psalmist David was facing several crises. What were they? How was the Lord sufficient for these critical needs?

2. Read Psalm 18:1–2. How is God described? What does this mean in your life?

3. In Psalm 40:2 David writes about how God rescued him. What did God do? Has he ever done this for you? When? How?

4. Psalm 62:1–2 describes God as a stabilizing force in our lives. According to these verses, what does he provide?

5. Matthew 5:1–12 lists several concepts that may seem upside down to you. After reading the passage, ask yourself the following questions: Who does God promise to bless? What blessing will come? When do you think it will happen? Why do you think these unlikely recipients receive special blessedness?

6. When you think about the character qualities mentioned in the previous verses, are there some that are under construction in your own life?

7. What is the difference between being "happy" and being "blessed"?

8. What are some things you have tried in your search for happiness and meaning? Did they provide what you were looking for?

9. God's will for our personal lives isn't meant to be obscure or mysterious. What do the following verses teach about knowing his will?
   • John 10:27
   • John 16:13
   • Romans 8:14
   • 1 Corinthians 2:16
   • 1 John 2:6

10. Take a few moments to consider your own life. Spiritually speaking, where are you? What are your needs? How can your needs be met? By this Bible study? By your involvement in a group? In a friendship with an older, more mature Christian? Pray for these needs and, as God leads, share them with someone else.

2

The Way Up Is Down

Dealing with Pride

For everyone who exalts himself will be humbled, and he who humbles himself will be exalted.

Luke 14:11

Women know the importance of advertisement, promotion, merchandising, and networking. And whether it's making a peanut butter sandwich, writing a book, or climbing the corporate ladder, we try to be the best we can be. So we educate ourselves, take steps that help us grow, and make plans for the future. But while we're trying to improve ourselves and promote our work, there's an inner voice reminding us, *Do not exalt yourself.* On the other hand, we are promised that when humility happens we "will be exalted."

Now I ask you, how confusing is that?

These concepts turn our minds completely upside down as we try to put the two together. What is humility, anyway? Are we to hang our heads, brush off every compliment, and constantly declare, "I am nothing" or "Let's just praise the Lord"? If I manage to appear humble or refuse an award when I know my work deserves recognition, is that humility? If I'm secretly longing for a raise or promotion, if I want my book to be a bestseller, if it feels good when my kids make the honor roll, does that mean I'm being prideful?

How in the world do we humble ourselves? And if we try to humble ourselves, the whole issue of motives comes up. If I want to be more humble so I can be exalted, isn't that the worst kind of pride?

Desiring to achieve something good while maintaining a selfless attitude is like trying to stay balanced on a narrow beam—chances are we'll eventually stumble and fall off one side or the other. Even if we manage to stay on top of that issue, pride sneaks up on us in other, more subtle ways. I hate to admit it, but occasionally I stumble during my most spiritual moments. Why, one morning after a particularly meaningful devotional time (of all things), I found myself thinking, *Wow, that was a really good prayer! What time is it, anyway?*

At other times pride creeps into my closest relationships. When conflicts arise, even when I know I should be the one to give in, there's something inside me that stands up and shouts, *It's not my fault! . . . I have every right . . . My way is best.* After a few minutes of that kind of self-talk, my emotions kick in and I feel imposed upon or misunderstood. I know it's hard to believe that a woman at my level of maturity (ahem . . . I'm speaking here in terms of years) has been known to whine or cry. Then I begin making choices that feed my ego, rather than honor God.

Can you identify with me? Perhaps you get caught up in the same emotional tug-of-war. You gain a measure of prestige, accomplish a significant task, reach a long-sought-after goal, and you're rightfully proud. Congratulations are in order! Then, before you can take a deep breath and stand up straight, something sinister happens and your head begins to grow. Instead of being grateful or considering your achievement a gift, you start thinking, *I am one creative female—a near genius. Look at what I have done.*

At least we're not alone as we try to tame this monster called pride. Throughout the centuries, saints have fought the battle before us. Andrew Murray, beloved devotional writer of the 1800s, described the struggle when he penned these words with wisdom and a touch of humor:

> Humility is that grace that, when you know you have it, you have lost it.

As you try to stay balanced, and if your conscience is well trained, you may be willing to acknowledge your missteps and confess them. Unfortunately for some, taking that step—a downward step that most Christians need to take daily—is late in coming. Pride becomes more than an occasional bout of self-ism and develops one overly confident step at a time into a way of life. When that happens, God often intervenes to bring about a change of heart. A case in point is King Nebuchadnezzar's rise to power in the kingdom of Babylon.

As the great king conquered nations and constructed wondrous palaces, temples, and gardens, he humbly acknowledged the God of Israel: "How great are His signs and how mighty are His wonders! His kingdom is an everlasting kingdom and His dominion is from generation to generation" (Dan. 4:3 NASB). Unfortunately, his

God-centered heart flip-flopped when he began to dwell on his own greatness, then started taking credit for it. Apparently, one night his "stinkin' thinkin'" wafted upward and offended the olfactory nerve of the Most High God. He interrupted King Neb's sleep with a really bad dream—one that warned of his coming downfall.

As destiny would have it, Daniel, one of several teenagers kidnapped in Jerusalem and carried off to Babylon to serve in the royal court, had displayed great wisdom. In fact, he'd become a confidant or counselor to the magistrate, one specializing in "dream therapy." This young squire understood Nebuchadnezzar's dream and interpreted it for him, warning him of the dangers of pride and bravely suggesting he change directions.[1] But in spite of Daniel's sage advice, the king continued scrambling upward on the so-called "ladder to success" without realizing the way up is down. A year later his awful dream became reality. Nebuchadnezzar slid into a state of madness.

The Bible records the train of thought that led the great monarch from a position of strength to a place of destruction. As the story goes, one day the king was strutting back and forth on the roof of the royal palace, reflecting on his many achievements. "Is this not Babylon the great, which I myself have built as a royal residence by the might of my power and for the glory of my majesty?" (Dan. 4:30 NASB).

"I myself"? "My power"? "My majesty"?

The Upside-Down Truth...

On the ladder to success, the way up is down.

That did it! Before he even finished his thought, God's voice boomed earthward, reverberating on celestial airwaves until it connected with his intended receiver—the ear of the proud king. "King Nebuchadnezzar, . . . sovereignty has been removed from you" (Dan. 4:31 NASB). Through the pen of Solomon, God told us to expect the same kind of outcome: "Pride goes before destruction, a haughty spirit before a fall" (Prov. 16:18). As we stumble through life, most of us could quote that promise, but not a single one of us want to claim it for ourselves.

Following what must have been a heart-stopping encounter with God, the king wandered out of his palace and into the fields where he lived for seven years, eating a unique variety of humble pie—the dew-drenched grasses of his own pasture. Once accustomed to the marble pools and baths of the palace, he now washed himself with dew and rain. His hair grew long "like eagles' feathers and his nails like birds' claws" (Dan. 4:33 NASB). I can't even imagine the angst this once dignified ruler must have felt as he grazed aimlessly year after year. But I must admit, the experiences he had make me want to humble *myself* before God has to do it for me. I don't think there's a woman among us who would not agree—especially when we think about that hair and fingernail thing!

It makes us feel better when we read that the king eventually came to himself. Somewhere in the wastelands, the once proud man took the most important step in his life—a downward step that led him back into a position of greatness. From the bottom rung of the ladder, he looked up and declared his allegiance to the Greatest King of all—the Most High God.

I, Nebuchadnezzar, raised my eyes toward heaven and my reason returned to me, and I blessed the Most High and praised and honored Him who lives forever;

For His dominion is an everlasting dominion,
And His kingdom endures from generation to
generation.
All the inhabitants of the earth are accounted as
nothing,
But He does according to His will in the host of
heaven
And among the inhabitants of earth;
And no one can ward off His hand
Or say to Him, "What have You done?" . . .

Now I, Nebuchadnezzar, praise, exalt and honor the King
of heaven, for all His works are true and His ways just, and
He is able to humble those who walk in pride.

Daniel 4:34–37 NASB

As he talks about his recovery, King Nebuchadnezzar
twice declares that his "reason returned" (Dan.
4:34, 36 NASB). Could it be that pride is a
sort of temporary insanity—a craziness
that claims we do not need God, that
we are self-sufficient? Is it possible
that we, as reasonably sane women,
could literally lose our minds the
way the good king did? That
possibility should strike fear in
every heart that's prone to think
of herself "more highly than [she]
ought" (Rom. 12:3). For what we
nonchalantly brush off as a minor
nuisance, calling it *just a little bit* of
pride, is a *really big* problem that can
actually drive us crazy. No wonder our
Father will deal with it, even if it causes
major discomfort to the child he loves.

Success is depending completely on God's grace; failure is depending on one's own accomplishments.

The Upside-Down Truth...

*T*here is one God; you are not Him!

Anonymous

A young woman I'll call Alex worked with me in a women's ministry. As our friendship grew, we shared dozens of lunches and laughed till our sides hurt over funny things that happened when we were together. We also had long talks about spiritual matters, including our latest insights from the Bible. But after a few months, I began to notice another side to my friend. If a complicated situation at church or some difference of opinion arose between us, she never, and I do mean never, faced up to her part of the problem. Instead she would deny, justify, or elaborately explain her actions, sometimes backing up her conclusions with Scripture.

There were times when I thought the gal was simply confused. At other times, her response seemed a bit crazy. But there were also times when I came away scratching my head, wondering if I was the crazy one. Eventually the crazy-making had to stop. Our friendship suffered irreconcilable differences, but in the meantime I learned a few important things about the insanity of pride.

The more a person tries to convince others they're right or that the situation is not what it seems, the more obvious it becomes how wrong they really are. Still, God never gives up on his wandering kids but is always working, lovingly, persistently, to bring them through fields overgrown with thorns and weeds into sunlight and lush green meadows.[2] Sometimes the process takes longer than seven years, and sometimes the story doesn't have a "happily ever after" ending. But if a person listens well and obeys God, amazing things happen—just as they did with King Nebuchadnezzar. Now that I think about this, I've got just one thing to say—well, maybe I've got two. *Yea, God! Bravo, King Neb!*

When he finally realized there was nothing good in himself, the king was filled with praise for the goodness of God.[3] Beforehand he had recognized *what* God had done for him—using his power to benefit Babylon, performing miracles, wonders, and signs. Afterward he praised God for *who* he is—eternal, supreme, sovereign, omnipotent, just. Is the king like some of the women you know? They love to see God's miracles and signs—especially when he's getting them out of a jam or giving them what they want. It takes a more mature woman to love God just because he is God.

After Nebuchadnezzar's sanity was restored, God reestablished his kingdom and his place of honor in Babylonian society. Then God was able to use him to literally change the course of history. Do you think it possible that God could do something extraordinary with gals like you and me? While you may hesitate to say yes, remember God's promise. His intention is not to simply bring us low so he can lord it over us. His plan is to exalt us. Mind-boggling things are in the works for our future—things that will honor him and bless our own lives as well. "Humble yourselves, therefore, under God's mighty hand, that he may lift you up in due time" (1 Peter 5:6).

"God resists, refuses, rejects the proud," writes Brennan Manning, "but he delivers himself up, he gives himself totally to the humble and the little. Not only does he not resist them, but he cannot refuse them anything."[4] A simple word search on my compu-Bible revealed several gifts that God gives. For one thing, he "gives us more grace" (James 4:6).

"Clothe yourselves with humility toward one another," wrote the apostle Peter, "because, 'God opposes the proud

but gives grace to the humble'" (1 Peter 5:5).
It's comforting to know that God's grace
equips us less-than-perfect women to
serve him. In fact, he even works our
failures into his plans. That's grace!
And as we "grow in the grace" as
well as in the knowledge of Jesus,
we will stop groveling, quit flaunt-
ing our God-given abilities, and
find many grace-opportunities
to accept women as they are and
minister to them "as good stew-
ards of the manifold grace of God"
(1 Peter 4:10 NASB).

> God assists
> the humble
> but resists
> the proud.

To clothe ourselves with humility
sounds so easy—like donning a new
blouse. In reality it's much more complicated. It's more like signing up for an extreme
makeover that begins with the heart. After all, what
we think about ourselves determines the kind of person we
become.[5] The woman who realizes God knows her completely—including all her faults, weaknesses, and sin—and
that he has forgiven her totally and freely, owes a debt she
can never repay. When she begins to bow, to simply say
thank you, she is well on the way toward being well dressed
in the garment of humility.

God also gives wisdom. "When pride comes, then comes
disgrace, but with humility comes wisdom" (Prov. 11:2).
Wisdom is much more than knowing facts, accumulating
data, stockpiling information. It's gaining insight, having tact, understanding people. Caryn, a well-informed
woman in my Bible study group, impressed me with her
wisdom. Even though she had acquired lots of info, she

didn't come across as a know-it-all. She possessed the rare quality of being a good listener and was learning not only *what* to do but *how* and *when* to do it—what to share, when to intervene, and most importantly, when to keep her mouth shut and do nothing. As I watched Caryn grow spiritually, I found myself wanting to be more like her—a little less interested in gathering information and a lot more focused on people and their needs. After all, most of us can absorb more facts than we'll ever use. What we really need is a double share of wisdom. And, surprising as it may seem, we don't have to share our two cents' worth on every issue.

---

each thy tongue to say, "I do not know."

Hebrew Proverb

The most important thing God provides is a way for us to have a deeper, fuller relationship with him—one that meets our most heartfelt needs. Another king of another era, the beloved David of Israel, wrote, "Though the LORD is on high, he looks upon the lowly, but the proud he knows from afar" (Ps. 138:6). Imagine God "on high" being in touch with the "lowly." Does that thought seem upside down to you? We don't have to be some sort of spiritual giant to get his attention or make an impression on him. In fact, the opposite is true. From his supreme place, God looks down, sees women who are small in their own eyes, and regards them as big. Then he invites us to know him better—as a friend knows a friend.

King Nebuchadnezzar has not been the only person of prominence to face up to his pride. The malady spans all positions, persons, and eras, and unfortunately, all levels of spiritual maturity. It even sneaks up on those who are closest to the Lord. The disciples who lived and worked side by side with Jesus struggled to keep their hearts free and centered on him.

On one occasion, Jesus told them a story to illustrate what humility and pride look like in everyday situations. Seems he was celebrating a Sabbath meal in the home of a well-known leader of the Pharisees. As the guests were taking their places at the table, Jesus couldn't help but notice how they were elbowing their way into the most prominent places. Maybe they wanted to be near him or seated by the host so they could hear everything that was said. It could have been they saw the dessert table and thought if they were close, they might be first in line. Whatever the reason, Jesus saw and took issue.

> When someone invites you to dinner, don't take the place of honor. Somebody more important than you might have been invited by the host. Then he'll come and call out in front of everybody, "You're in the wrong place. The place of honor belongs to this man." Red-faced, you'll have to make your way to the very last table, the only place left.
>
> When you're invited to dinner, go and sit at the last place. Then when the host comes he may very well say, "Friend, come up to the front." That will give the dinner guests something to talk about! What I'm saying is, If you walk around with your nose in the air, you're going to end up flat on your face. But if you're content to be simply yourself, you will become more than yourself.
>
> Luke 14:8–11 Message

I know what you are thinking: *That would never happen in my circle of friends. Nobody's that self-centered or mean-spirited.* The truth is, it happens! That scene has been replayed in groups of women throughout the centuries.

One Saturday morning I watched a similar drama unfold at a spring luncheon in my hometown. The woman in
charge of decorations shrugged her shoulders and grinned
as she put her own place card at the head table. As she
brushed her hands on her jeans, I overheard her say, "It's
my own little reward for a decorating job well done." She
must have known that taking the place near the speaker
left no room for a woman I'll call Kellie who had led the
steering committee.

When the guests arrived, Kellie reacted to the seating
arrangement with an extra measure of grace. She quietly
took a seat at a nearby table, and just as he promised, God
exalted her. She didn't get to sit by the speaker, she didn't
get a standing ovation when she introduced him, there was
no winning lottery ticket taped to the bottom of her chair,
but she was honored. She won a place of respect not only
in my heart but in the hearts of many others, including
the young women in the Sunday school class she taught
who couldn't help but notice the intentional snubbing. In
the process, they learned a bit about the humiliation that
comes when a woman exalts herself. "A [woman's] pride
brings [her] low," Solomon wrote, "but a [woman] of lowly
spirit gains honor" (Prov. 29:23).

The story that Jesus told, translated in such an easy-
to-understand way by Eugene Peterson in *The Message*,
concludes by describing a humble person as "content to be
simply yourself" (Luke 14:11). Is humility simply "being
yourself"—being completely and honestly who or what
God created you to be?

The apostle Paul encourages us to think of ourselves
"with sober judgment" (Rom. 12:3)—with sound, proper
thinking, not having thoughts exaggerated one way or
another. Not putting on airs or trying to impress people

with some sort of feigned importance. Not building walls to protect ourselves or to hide our true self from others. Humility is not having a low opinion of ourselves; it is having an accurate opinion—seeing ourselves through God's eyes.

An accurate opinion means not entertaining self-deprecating thoughts—*I am a worm and should spend the rest of my life crawling in the mud on my belly*. It is not thinking lofty New Age thoughts—*I am like God*, or *I am becoming a god*. The right opinion is knowing we are somewhere between these two extremes: I am a woman for whom Christ died, a woman of worth, with gifts, talents, and abilities of great value in the kingdom of God, yet I am weak and capable of misusing what God has given to exalt myself rather than to honor him.

If you're content to be simply yourself,
you will become more than yourself.

Stephen Arterburn

In *More Jesus, Less Religion* Stephen Arterburn writes about some little kids who posted a sign on their clubhouse door. Without knowing it, they expressed with their simple words an insight into humility that's hard for us grown-ups to match. Scribbled boldly in block lettering the sign proclaimed, "Nobody Act Big, Nobody Act Small, Everybody Act Medium."[6] As I've settled into that comfortable place—just being me, contentedly happily "medium"—I've been able to get a grip on what it means to "become more" than myself.

"The proud hilltops let the rain run off," Augustine wrote, "and the lowly valleys are richly watered." As we settle down and make our home in the fertile valleys of humility, the jagged peaks towering above remind us of the barrenness of self-centered lives.

I can only imagine the succulent fruit that grows in the good soil of the vale. But if we search for it, I'm sure we will find several varieties of grace, a bounty of wisdom, abundant honor, and much more. So meet me at the foothills and let's join hands as we harvest the fruit. Bring a big basket and wear comfortable clothes, for I'm sure we'll have to bend low to gather it.

Right-Side Up

1. How do you define success?

2. What biblical insights have helped form your opinion?

3. According to Henri Frederic Amiel, "True humility is contentment." What are your thoughts about this statement? Does it define humility for you? Why or why not?

4. Is feeling inadequate an asset or handicap? Explain your answer.

5. Read Philippians 2:5–11. In these verses Paul writes about the humiliation of Christ. He is our supreme example, showing us how to deal with our "rights" or with inner feelings of pride. The passage begins, "Your attitude should be the same as that of Christ Jesus." What was his attitude?

6. What do you discover in each of the following verses?
   • Proverbs 22:4
   • Isaiah 29:19
   • Jeremiah 45:5a
   • Proverbs 22:1

7. Read Philippians 4:2–3. Apparently these two
   women could not agree with each other. Have you
   ever been in a women's group where there was
   some sort of discord? Do you think pride contrib-
   utes to the problem? Is growth in humility part of
   the solution?

3

Whoever Is Last Will Be First

Handling Competition and Comparisons

If anyone wants to be first, he must be the very last, and the servant of all.

Mark 9:35

In all my wanderings through the Christian community, I've not found one woman who really wants to be last. Never heard a single one admit she relishes losing the race, fumbling the ball, or winning the white ribbon. Nope, nary a one! In fact, I've come to conclude there's something, inborn in all of us, that pushes us onward, upward, toward excellence. We want to win, make a difference, be influential, change the condition of our world. Maybe it's because we want to be like Jesus, who, after all, has been declared "first place in everything" (Col. 1:18 NASB). Actually there's nothing wrong, and lots of things right, about wanting to be first.

So what did our First Place Lord mean when he told his disciples that the "first will be last and the last first"? Why did he insist, "Whoever wants to become great . . . must be your servant" (Mark 10:43)? Is this the kind of ministry he exemplified to his followers? How did he train them? How does this message, which seems upside down to our natural minds, apply to the right-side-up, everyday realities of a woman's life?

For one thing, I think Jesus wanted us to take a good hard look at what it takes (or does *not* take) to make a positive impact in this world. You certainly don't have to have Wonder Woman strength or Miss Congeniality charm. Serving Jesus is much easier than that. Maybe it's just making the most of your own God-given strengths as well as your weaknesses. In some ways, it's simply doing what comes naturally—or what comes supernaturally.

Some of us come into this world with an up-front, take-charge personality. From the time we learned to hopscotch, we've been the ones to draw the lines and tell everybody else how to jump. Since I fall into this category, I find it hard to understand my laid-back counterparts. Still, I'm told there are some who are quite content to follow, to simply be a part of the crowd.

If you are energetic about spiritual matters, you've probably had a group of

The Upside-Down Truth...

God doesn't call the qualified; he qualifies the called.

close friends, family members, or mentors cheering you on from the sidelines. Sometimes these cheerleaders are just glad to have somebody, *anybody*, do the work that needs to be done. (Or maybe do the work they don't want to do!) Others are more sincere. Take the youth minister of my church when I was a teen. "Someday," he began with a faraway look on his face, "I think God will use you to teach his Word. You have a good speaking voice; I can just see you being a leader."

Hmmm. I liked that idea.

What he said about my voice was verified by something my mother said the very next day when I was talking to a group of girlfriends. "Gracie," she began gently, "your voice carries. I know you didn't want me to hear what you said, but I did hear—every word. You'd better be careful!" I cringed as I tried to remember exactly what I'd just blurted. Even today, decades later, I remember my mom's reproof and try to manage what I say as well as the decibel level of my inner boom box.

Unfortunately, that wasn't the only time words got me in trouble as I was growing up. Nevertheless, somewhere in the back of my mind, I knew they could also be used for good. In those early years, I liked memorizing Scripture. Besides that, I thought putting a few righteous words into my memory banks just might offset some of my off-beat verbal withdrawals. Sometimes, when I had learned a few verses word perfect, I'd be asked to quote them before the entire congregation. I still remember gripping the sides of the big oak pulpit, not about to let anybody know there were butterflies fluttering in my tummy. Thankfully I matured, and as destiny would have it, doors eventually opened for me to teach other women some of what I had learned.

As soon as I became loud-mouthed-leader-in-charge, I had to do something about the butterflies. So I subscribed to *Leadership Magazine* and read an article on how I could be the leader I was meant to be. I also signed up for a speaker's seminar where I learned to use an outline and develop illustrations. With the new info, my confidence grew. Whoopee! I was ready to change the world.

Imagine how I felt when one day in a quiet moment, I read these words: "If anyone wants to be first, he must be the very last, and the servant of all" (Mark 9:35).

Impossible!

How can anybody lead from last place? Why, if I'm standing at the back of the room or at the end of the line, nobody will even notice me. My second thought came from a deeper place in me—that spiritual place where God communicates with the human soul. *Maybe, just maybe, serving God is not about being up front or in charge. Perhaps it's more about what happens behind the scenes when no one is watching. Isn't that what being a "servant" means?*

My subsequent thoughts centered on the leadership style (or rather the servant-ship style) of Jesus. Our Lord—the only one who truly deserves to be in first place—never pushed his way to the front. In fact, he rarely spoke to large groups of people. Ducking away from the crowds, he often pulled his disciples aside for a bit of tutoring. And he served those he loved by doing the most mundane tasks, like washing their feet and cooking fish over an open fire for their breakfast.[1]

At least I'm not the only strong-willed disciple who has needed a midcourse correction! The original twelve had to face their wrong concepts about serving God too. On one occasion Peter, James, and John had just come down from the mountaintop—both literally and spiritually. They had seen Jesus's human body take on a heavenly glow as white and bright as a bolt of lightning, and they'd heard God's voice boom overhead, "This is my Son, whom I love. Listen to him!" (Mark 9:7). One can only imagine what they must have felt as they huddled together on that mountain.

But, after descending to the foothills and walking several miles through Galilee and on toward Capernaum, the disciples found that the heavenly experience had faded a bit and a few earthly, very human thoughts played about in their minds. I suppose they were excited about the ministry of Jesus and wanted to be included, to get involved, to make a difference. Most of us who love Jesus today feel the same passion. But their good intentions took a nosedive when they began arguing among themselves about who would get the most prominent position in this important work.

Jesus overheard them.

My heart goes out to those guys. They must have had voices that carry and a mother who didn't warn them!

Once they were settled in a house in Capernaum, Jesus decided it was time to expose what was going on in their hearts. He addressed the matter. "What were you arguing about on the road?" (Mark 9:33). They must have looked like a bunch of kids in big trouble as the Lord gazed past their wide-eyed expressions into their very souls.

I can just see them shuffling their feet as their eyes darted back and forth, each wondering if the other was willing to fess up. Then they did what most of us would have done: they shrugged their shoulders and kept their mouths shut.[2] But Jesus didn't let the matter rest. He gathered the entire group in the living room and said something that turned their minds upside down. "He who is least among you all—he is the greatest" (Luke 9:48).

The beginning of greatness is to be little.
The increase of greatness is to be less.
The perfection of greatness is to be nothing.

D. L. Moody

I wish I could tell you this was the only time Jesus had to confront this issue. On another occasion James and John even got their mother into a discussion about their place in the future kingdom. Jesus, knowing full well what was going on in their hearts, looked directly into the eyes of the concerned mom and asked, "What do you wish?" (Matt. 20:21 NASB).

Emboldened by his question, Salome revealed the desire of her heart. "Command that in Your kingdom these two sons of mine may sit one on Your right and one on Your left" (v. 22 NASB).

Now, I know what you are thinking. *How could she? How selfish!* Or, if you're in tune with today's Christian catch phrases, you might shrug your shoulders, turn your palms up, and declare, *Hel-lo! It's not about you!* You may also be tempted to respond like the other ten disciples did. Apparently an all-out tug-of-war began when they found out what the two had wanted.[3]

Jesus settled the argument by calling them to gather round. I imagine the Lord putting his arms around a couple of big, burly necks and explaining to the group once again in simple terms, using an example they could easily understand. "You know that the rulers of the Gentiles lord it over them, and their great men exercise authority over them. It is not this way among you, but whoever wishes to become great among you shall be your servant, and whoever wishes to be first among you shall be your slave"

(Matt. 20:25–27 NASB). The mission of Jesus's followers in those early days, as well as in our ministry today, would need to be radically different from that of the nonbelieving world. Before the circle broke and the men headed toward Jericho, Jesus reminded them why he came in the first place. "The Son of Man did not come to be served, but to serve, and to give His life a ransom for many" (Matt. 20:28 NASB).

> Great people are not lords; great people are servants.

How many times would Jesus have to explain before the disciples would get it? How can we expect Salome, a loving, doting mother, to understand? Even the disciples, who were with Jesus every day, didn't grasp the amazing, upside-down truth.

Before you get too judgmental about Salome's request, think about your own family. Wouldn't you want your children to be close to Jesus? Do you want somebody else's child to be closer to the Lord than your own? I have no problem identifying with this mother. I want my sons to be intimate with the Lord—more in tune with his will and purposes than any other man on earth.

I appreciate Salome's desire to see her sons in first place. The problem is, she got ahead of herself—actually, she got ahead of God. All of us are destined to reign with God in heaven.[4] Even now, as we live out our days we feel that pull toward heavenly places.[5] But before we can take our first-place position in God's future kingdom, we must do our time in second place here on planet Earth.

Isn't Salome's problem one all we women share? We run ahead of God. We're impatient. We want what's coming to us, and we want it now. We're especially impatient and sometimes more than a little presumptuous when it comes to the spiritual growth or advancement of our children. We may take heart when we realize that God has a plan for all our kids, just as he did for Salome's. Look at what Jesus said: "Just as My Father has granted Me a kingdom, I grant you that you may eat and drink at My table in My kingdom, and you will sit on thrones judging the twelve tribes of Israel" (Luke 22:29–30 NASB).

When Jesus explained to Salome, "It is not mine to give," he was honoring the eternal plan of God. Only God the Father knows the plans he has, not only for Salome and her boys, but for all of us. "'I know the plans I have for you,' declares the LORD, 'plans to prosper you and not to harm you, plans to give you hope and a future'" (Jer. 29:11). God himself will reveal his plans, but only at the right time. In the meantime, we need to accept, maybe even learn to enjoy, being in last place.

God is never late. But He misses a lot
of great opportunities to be early.
Jeanette Clift-George

One of the passages I memorized when I was a girl was the Beatitudes.[6] My mother said that the name described the way my "attitude" ought to "be." It's a passage that can turn upside-down thinking completely right-side up. For in these verses we see what kind of person and which positions on earth are truly esteemed by God. Every verse begins with the word "blessed"—a word that means a lot more than "happiness." It describes a state of being that's extremely fortunate or well-off. None of it really makes much sense to most of us, for this kind of "blessedness" is promised to the most unlikely recipients.

As illogical as it may sound, Jesus said, "Blessed are the poor in spirit" (Matt. 5:3). This literally means "blessed are the paupers." It is another way of saying that those who are insignificant, those who escape our notice, those who possess little or nothing in this world are the ones who are truly blessed. Can that really be true? Oswald Chambers, beloved devotional writer of another era, seems to think so. He wrote, "The foundation of Jesus Christ's kingdom is the genuine loveliness of those who are commonplace."[7] Does God reserve his choice blessings for "commonplace" or second-place people?

If so, we need to change our way of thinking.

Unfortunately, change comes slowly for most of us, just as it did for the early disciples. Near the end of Jesus's earthly ministry, he and his disciples were celebrating the Passover meal in the upper room. As the disciples arrived, Jesus bowed before them, one by one, and washed their feet. He served the Passover meal and talked to them about his impending suffering, death, and resurrection. It must have been the most solemn occasion the guys had ever experienced, the most obvious example of Christian service they'd ever seen. But the slow-to-understand men completely missed the point. They'd no sooner folded their napkins and pushed back from the table than the after-dinner conversation turned to (of all things) who would get to be in first place. "Within minutes they were bickering over who of them would end up the greatest" (Luke 22:24 Message).

Jesus must have been shaking his head as he explained, "Kings like to throw their weight around and people in authority like to give themselves fancy titles. It's not going to be that way with you. Let the senior among you become like the junior; let the elder act the part of the servant" (Luke 22:25–26 Message).

Unfortunately, I have no room to criticize the disciples. I'd been teaching women's Bible studies several years before a humiliating experience taught me what serving others is all about.

After an extended illness, I was eager to teach my group again. I arrived early with a big smile on my face. I had notified a woman I'll call Lucy who'd been teaching in my place, but when I walked to the front, her Bible and notebook were already resting on the speaker's stand. My smile turned upside down as I walked to the back of the room and put my books on a chair. When it was time to begin, Lucy welcomed me back, introduced a new series, and proceeded to teach the lesson. *She had taken over my group!*

For several weeks after that, I felt hurt as I puzzled over what to do. Eventually, I started a new group, but my unsettled feelings continued. I grieved the loss of my old group, my former ministry. Even though both groups flourished, I couldn't enjoy the success. My resentment toward Lucy grew.

Then one morning I got a glimpse of myself from God's perspective. Running late, I dropped off my kids at school, careened around a corner, and pulled into the church's parking lot. I jumped from my car right into a huge puddle. Before I reached the building, a gust of wind caught the plastic wrap covering the heart-shaped cake I carried. My hairdo flipped backward and my umbrella turned inside out, allowing rain to drizzle down my back. When I burst through the door, there stood Lucy dressed in a navy suit, dark hose, and high heels. She was talking with our pastor and taking notes in her burgundy leather folder with her matching burgundy pen.

Unbelievable!

I brushed past them as I headed toward my classroom. Then I noticed a huge smear of pink icing on my denim dress and mud on my tennis shoes. *Why did I wear this? Why am I so clumsy?* Somehow I gained my composure, taught my class, and served soggy cake. Then I hurried home and spent all afternoon doing some serious soul searching.

I thought of other times in my life when I'd felt inadequate and times when I'd struggled to be the best I could be. I examined my motives. Was I teaching because I loved God or simply because I liked to teach—because I was good at it, because it met a need in my own life, making me feel more important, more whole? Whose work was I doing, after all? Was it really *my* group? As the hours slipped by and I continued to pray and think, I found myself wondering if it were more spiritual, somehow more holy, to be the teacher of Bible studies, or to deliver a loaf of bread to a sick neighbor. Was it more in tune with God's will for me to stand before a group and speak, or to whisper quiet words into the ear of a hurting friend?

Of course the answer became obvious. The holiest thing I could do, or that any one of us can do, is exactly what our holy heavenly Father asks at the time. It might mean teaching, or it might mean serving bread, or . . . it might mean washing feet. In the years since, I've taught many Bible studies, but there have also been times when I have not—quiet times, alone times, times of service that nobody knows anything about, and times when my emotional energy has dried up. But in all those times, I have learned to be content. And I am blessed. "You're blessed when you're content with just who you are—no more, no less. That's the moment you find yourselves proud owners of everything that can't be bought" (Matt. 5:5 Message).

So what about the service I rendered in the name of ministry during those early days? How will my work be evaluated when the righteous Judge hands out his blue ribbons? Hopefully, truth came through even during those misdirected days and some lives may have been changed.[8] Meanwhile, as I finish the course God has laid out for me, I leave the results to him. And I'm encouraged when I realize I'm not the only disciple who's stumbled as we walk along the way.

None struggled more to understand the message and ministry of Jesus than Peter. Peter the fisherman, the impetuous water walker, the disciple who slept when he promised to pray, the one who denied his Lord. But this is the same man who later wrote, "Be shepherds of God's flock that is under your care, serving as overseers . . . as God wants you to be; . . . eager to serve; not lording it over those entrusted to you, but being examples to the flock" (1 Peter 5:2–3). Apparently somewhere between the blunders of his early discipleship and the writing of his two letters preserved in the New Testament, Peter learned a thing or two about loving and serving others. Perhaps he finally got it when Jesus called him aside for an intimate conversation. It took place after Jesus's death and resurrection. The disciples had gathered on the shore of Galilee where Jesus cooked breakfast over an open fire. When they had finished eating, Jesus jumped into the life-changing dialogue with a point-blank question.

"Simon, son of John, do you love me more than these?"
"Yes, Master, you know I love you."
Jesus said, "Feed my lambs."

He then asked a second time, "Simon, son of John, do you love me?"

"Yes, Master, you know I love you."

Jesus said, "Shepherd my sheep."

Then he said it a third time: "Simon, son of John, do you love me?"

Peter was upset that he asked for the third time, "Do you love me?" so he answered, "Master, you know everything there is to know. You've got to know that I love you."

Jesus said, "Feed my sheep."

John 21:15–17 Message

The story is familiar to most of us, but it doesn't make much sense until we know what these two men were really saying to each other. The ultimate example of male miscommunication, Peter was replying with a totally different word for *love* than the one Jesus had used. In essence this is what they said:

"Peter," Jesus asked, "do you love me with unconditional, agape love? Do you love me unselfishly, sacrificially, enough to give your life for me?"

"You know how much I love you, Lord," Peter answered, using a word that expresses less than to-die-for allegiance. "Why, I love you like a brother. We share the same interests."

I wonder what feelings registered on Jesus's face as he posed the question again. Regret? Frustration? Disappointment? Sadness? "Do you love me unconditionally with agape love?" he asked. "Do you love me unselfishly, sacrificially?"

"Lord, you know I'm your friend," Peter reiterated. "We have a lot in common."

At this point, Jesus got down on Peter's very human level and rephrased the question with the same word Peter had used to define their relationship. "So, do you consider me your friend, Peter? Do we have common interests and goals?"

Apparently the slow-to-comprehend disciple finally got it. The Bible says Peter was grieved because Jesus had asked three times, "Do you love me?" I imagine Peter swallowing hard as he answered honestly. "Lord, you know all things. You see things full circle, from a perspective high above what I can comprehend. Besides that, you know by experience that I am your friend. Remember all the times I have befriended you? We share the same interests."

I find it interesting that Jesus not only questioned Peter's love for him again and again and again, but each time he repeated the command "feed my sheep." Actually he told Peter to "shepherd" them, a word that means much more than to "feed." It includes standing guard, protecting the lambs from wolves and lions, guiding them into the fold, providing clear water and good pasture. Why would Jesus ask the faltering disciple to care for his sheep? Why did he press the issue three times?

Was he just out to reveal his disciple's faults? Or was he accomplishing something much deeper? Could it be that Jesus wanted Peter to know his own heart, to see how weak and powerless he was? Perhaps Jesus wanted Peter to be absolutely convinced of his less-than-first-place status so that eventually he could be exalted.

Whatever the lesson Jesus intended, Peter must have learned it well. He is the most prominent character in the New Testament, mentioned more times than any follower of Christ. After Jesus ascended to heaven, Peter, a simple fisherman, a man who had failed again and again, a man who didn't know what love is, would preach of God's redeeming love to the crowd gathered for the feast of Pentecost. Over three thousand people would believe in Jesus after hearing his message. He would go on to serve Jesus in a fruitful ministry that would build the early church and establish it in truth. The man whose name meant "little stone" became a "rock" faithfully representing the Rock of Ages.

Could it also be that Jesus pressed the issue because he wanted to make a clear point for future disciples, including women like you and me? One that would be preserved in a story passed down through the centuries—a story that would help us love Jesus more and encourage us to be good shepherds, even though we might do it imperfectly.

How many times does he have to tell us before we get it?

God uses less-than-perfect individuals so that it is obvious to all that everything praiseworthy comes from a power greater than ourselves.

So, if you are still interested in finding a place of service for God, then join me. Right here at the back of the line.

Right-Side Up

1. Read the parable of the landowner in Matthew
   20:1–16. Apparently the laborers hired at first were
   unable to harvest the grapes and get them into the
   barn before dark. Four times the landowner went
   into the marketplace to recruit additional workers.
   When it was time to pay the laborers, whom did
   he pay first? How much did he pay them? Was this
   fair? Why or why not?

2. Read 1 Corinthians 2:1–5. Did Paul have a good
   speaking voice? Did he have self-confidence? What
   exactly were his qualifications for ministry? What
   was his message?

3. In 1 Peter 1:22, the apostle Peter wrote: "Now that
   you have purified yourselves by obeying the truth
   so that you have sincere love for your brothers, love
   one another deeply, from the heart." To describe
   the kind of love future disciples would need, he
   used the same two words that he once had trouble
   distinguishing between in his conversation with the
   risen Lord (see John 21:15–17). Look up the word in
   a concordance and record your findings. What does
   this teach you about Peter's spiritual growth?

4. First Peter 1:8 reveals a mature love for Jesus. What
   does the verse say? Describe this kind of love.
   What is required for us to love Jesus this way?

5. According to 1 Peter 4:8–11, what is required for spiritual service to God and others?

6. Think about your personal criteria for a leader, teacher, or minister. Examine the following points and consider how your point of view differs from God's.

When we fill a leadership position, we may think the job requires
- a person with leadership skills;
- a woman who's strong—having inner strength, physical energy, and good health;
- a person with an impressive educational background, educated in the best schools and universities—preferably Christian schools;
- a woman who is self-confident;
- a woman with a vibrant and outgoing personality;
- a woman who loves God supremely—with all her heart.

When God looks for a person to lead his people, he looks for someone with qualities that seem completely upside down to us! He seeks
- a woman who knows she's inadequate so she will depend on him;
- a woman who realizes she's weak so she will be empowered by God's resources—his Word, prayer, fellowship with other believers, godly counsel with accountability;

- one who may or may not have a college education, but one who values spiritual truth; one who
  knows that only God's truth sets a person free;
- a woman who is not self-confident, but one who
  finds her confidence in Christ; she is lost and
  empty without him, but secure and complete in
  him;
- a woman whose personality may not be dynamic,
  but who reflects his grace, love, and peace;
- a person who knows her own heart—one who
  can confess, "Yes, I love God, but even my love
  for him is affected by my flesh. I am growing in
  my love for him as I know him better."

～4～

In Giving We Receive

Managing Financial Blessings
with Freedom and Grace

Give, and it will be given to you. A good measure, pressed down, shaken together and running over, will be poured into your lap.

Luke 6:38

Extending our hand to the needy while expecting a gift in return is a concept that seems upside down to most of us. For one thing, it violates the whole spirit of giving. We've been taught from childhood that having such expectations is not only selfish but downright rude. So what did Jesus mean when he said, "Give and it shall be given to you"? If I give generously, can I expect a financial windfall? Will I receive riches enough to fill my lap and spill over onto the floor? That's what this verse *seems* to claim.

The passage goes on to say, "For with the measure you use, it will be measured to you" (Luke 6:38c). Does that mean that when you give money, you will get equal cash back? Maybe you'll get even more than you gave away. If that's so, then giving is a nice way to pad your bank account—a good investment that promises steady growth and huge dividends. Perhaps we all should "give" toward retirement rather than saving for it. Maybe instead of putting aside money for a new home, we should give our present house to a needy family, then stand back and wait for a bigger one to be presented to us, maybe in a better neighborhood with better schools. If we are assured of receiving an equal measure of goods to compensate every gift, then it doesn't matter whether or not we can afford it. We should give lavishly with no consideration of what it costs—a sort of blind faith agreement with God. Right?

I don't think so!

Perhaps I could accept such teaching at face value were it not for other biblical instruction that tells us to give "without expecting to get anything back" (Luke 6:35). And what about personal experiences that confirm a different reality? Take, for example, the experience our friends Larry and Marilyn had during one sweltering-hot Texas summer. Highly motivated by a powerful sermon that promised a "double miracle" to those who would make a double offering, Larry gave twice as much as usual, including the money he and his wife had set aside for the electric bill.

As he dropped a handful of folded bills in the offering plate at church, he fully expected money from an unknown source to arrive back home, and just in the knick of time. Unfortunately, instead of experiencing a miracle, his power was cut off—in more ways than one. As he and Marilyn sat in their living room fanning each other with folded newspapers, Larry felt completely helpless, frustrated, and ashamed. Did he misunderstand God? Did he give too much? Was his timing off? Did he not have enough faith?

A few days later, Larry rethought his "giving to get" theology. A lightbulb flashed in his head as he and Marilyn read from the New Testament: "Each man should give what he has decided in his heart to give" (2 Cor. 9:7).

"Well, who'd uh thunk it!" Larry quipped. "Giving should be based on a decision—a clearheaded choice—instead of impulse!" Marilyn grinned as Larry continued to read, "'. . . not reluctantly or under compulsion, for God loves a cheerful giver.'"

"Well," he sighed, "I guess that's why we're sweating this one out—and the pun is intended!" Larry wiped sweat from his brow and shook his head as he felt guilty on all three counts—feeling reluctant; acting under pressure; and feeling more than a little smug instead of cheerful.

Perhaps Larry would have grasped the meaning more quickly and clearly had he been reading from Eugene Peterson's easy-to-understand version, *The Message*. "I want each of you to take plenty of time to think it over, and make up your own mind what you will give. That will protect you against sob stories and arm-twisting. God loves it when the giver delights in the giving."

Most of us, at one time or another, can identify with Larry. We act emotionally when the needs are great and the pressures hot. Still, in spite of our mistakes, the Bible encourages giving by promising some sort of reward. Solomon, the wise king of Israel, wrote, "He who is kind to the poor lends to the LORD, and he will reward him for what he has done" (Prov. 19:17). The apostle Paul wrote, "Remember this: Whoever sows sparingly will also reap sparingly, and whoever sows generously will also reap generously" (2 Cor. 9:6). Sounds like our bigheartedness will definitely reap benefits, but what kind of return can we expect—financial blessings, better comprehension of God's truth, more understanding of people and their problems, the gift of grace? Or . . . all of the above?

For several years, I worked at Cherry's Christian Bookstore in my hometown of Greenville, Texas. While waiting on customers and stocking bookshelves, I couldn't help but notice the generosity of the store's owner. Cherry dispensed the good medicine of truth by handing out hundreds of gospel tracts and booklets on God's faithfulness. She often gave away books and Bibles. Occasionally she felt led to give money. Cherry said, "Some of the greatest blessings of my life have come because I gave to someone else." Cherry reaped a generous harvest, just as Scripture promises. But her "gifts" came in all sorts of odd-shaped packages, often delivered in surprising ways.

We don't give to get; we get to give.

Were there financial blessings? Yes! It seemed to me the store prospered all the more because of Cherry's benevolence. But the return on her spiritual investment was not so she could become a rich businesswoman. Her financial well-being enabled her to give to needy people again and again. "And God is able to make all grace abound to you, so that in all things at all times, having all that you need, you will abound in every good work" (2 Cor. 9:8). When I read these verses I can't help but notice the emphasis on the word "all"—*all* grace, *all* things, at *all* times, *all* that you need. Now I ask you, how complete and *all*-encompassing is that promise? But this abundant supply of resources is not for personal gain but for "every good work." And, as long as Cherry owned the bookstore, her good work continued.

One winter morning I watched as a woman wearing a long coat and white sandals pushed through the door and began sorting through the books near the front counter. Since the bookstore is located near the bus station, passengers frequently wandered in, looking for a handout. But something about this woman was different. Though obviously needy, she didn't ask for money. When she spotted Cherry, her request exposed a need of the heart. "Can someone pray for me?" Cherry kindly escorted her into the office, where she talked with her and prayed for her. Then she selected a leather study Bible, imprinted the woman's name on it, and presented it to her. The woman literally skipped out the door. Cherry's reward was in knowing that she had helped one of God's children carry a heavy load.

On another occasion, Cherry reaped an amazing spiritual return from a relatively small investment of money. During our coffee-break conversation, she told me about a young man named David who came in the store one day peddling dishes. When Cherry said she didn't need any, he seemed more than a little disappointed. The guy ducked his head and muttered, "If I don't sell something today, I won't have enough money to get back home." The man's humility impressed Cherry. She gave him twenty dollars to buy gas. David was elated as he asked, "How can I ever repay you?" Cherry couldn't hold back a smile as she suggested, "Well . . . , if you really want to repay me, come back after you buy the gasoline and let me tell you about Jesus."

In less than half an hour, David returned.

Cherry's heart beat at a faster-than-usual pace as she explained the gospel to him. He believed every word and responded sincerely by asking Jesus to forgive his sin and change his life. Then with tears pooling in his eyes, David revealed something Cherry will never forget. "When I parked in front of your store a couple of hours ago, I looked up toward the sky and whispered, 'God, if you are real, I need help.'" David dabbed his eyes with a tissue as a broad grin spread across his face. "Now, I know he is real!"

"That," Cherry declared, "was one of the greatest blessings I ever received. There's no reward bigger than that!"

Not every giving experience produced the same kind of fruit, nor did Cherry always feel blessed in the process. But, even when her blessing basket did not overflow, even when she felt she'd been used, Cherry recognized an opportunity to simply trust God, a time to grow in faith. "Sometimes it's hard to know when to give and when not to give," she admitted, "but my only responsibility is to the Lord. You know, we are never responsible for the behavior of someone else."

Not everything that counts can be counted,
not everything that can be counted counts.

Albert Einstein

Cherry is not the only one who comes face-to-face with the poor. Their needs are obvious and, to be honest, a bit overwhelming to most people, including members of our family. Homeless people live under bridges, loiter in parks and doorways, or hang out near the Austin Street Shelter in nearby Dallas. Panhandlers meander along the streets of downtown Fort Worth. Poverty-stricken men and women congregate under the overpass near the college campus where our son attends school. As Christians who've received so much from our benevolent heavenly Father, we are touched. Having freely received, we long to freely give.[1] But we can't help them all. Our heads spin crazily as we try to sort out the questions that pop into our minds. Will our gifts enable bad behavior? What really helps? The Bible offers guidelines, but frankly they seem a bit topsy-turvy to us.

It's easy for us to give to family members or friends who are struggling. We often help people hurt by natural disasters or tragedies. But Jesus taught his followers to give to the most undeserving people, including their enemies and those who hated them, even those who would curse, mistreat, or steal from them.[2] He asked them not to judge or condemn but to extend grace and forgiveness.[3] Did Jesus really mean "Give to everyone who asks you, and if anyone takes what belongs to you, do not demand it back" (Luke 6:30)? Those words cause all sorts of mental gymnastics. Am I supposed to give to *everybody* who asks—the beggar on the street corner or the woman who refuses to get a job? Sometimes? Every time I'm asked? How much?

How confusing!

But, in the same conversation with his disciples, Jesus said some things easy to understand—words that inspire generous giving even when it doesn't make sense. He reminds them that "the Most High . . . is kind to the ungrateful and wicked" (Luke 6:35). He tells them to "be merciful, just as your Father is merciful" (Luke 6:36). Perhaps most significantly, it is in the context of such unexplainable giving that Jesus established the Golden Rule—a standard of conduct that has guided people of all faiths throughout the centuries: "Do to others as you would have them do to you" (Luke 6:31).

Perhaps it was the Golden Rule that guided our young adult son, Jason, one evening as he strolled through the Dallas Arts District. An old derelict approached him, begging for a handout. "Just a buck for food?" he muttered.

"You don't really want something to eat, do you?" Jason responded skeptically. "Why not tell the truth?"

A long silence followed before the bum stammered, "I . . . I need a drink."

Jason paused, then in a moment of compassion, saw past the old man's wrinkled face with its smudges and stubbly whiskers and got a glimpse into his soul. He decided to respect the man's honesty. Dispensing grace instead of judgment, he pressed two dollars into the man's hand. Does that kind of benevolence seem upside down to you? Is it possible that God could, or would, use something as questionable as a drink to accomplish his purposes? At the thought of that, most of us throw up our hands and declare, *I honestly don't know!*

Before you make a judgment call, remember the occasions that Jesus was "moved with compassion" toward undeserving recipients of his grace. He didn't meet every need that he encountered but followed his Father's will, motivated by love.[4] Is it possible that women like you and me, or guys like Jason, represent him best when we simply follow his lead, opening our hands and our hearts?[5] The aging apostle John expressed this when he wrote, "If anyone has material possessions and sees his brother in need but has no pity on him, how can the love of God be in him?" (1 John 3:17). According to Jason,

Charity gives itself rich; greed hoards itself poor.

God did something good for both the giver and receiver that night in Dallas. "As crazy as it may sound," he began, "I think God used me that day—maybe just to show his unconditional love." Jason grinned and added, "Anyway, my conscience was clear."

There are two kinds of people in the world—
givers and takers,
Sometimes the takers eat better,
but the givers sleep better.

Danny Thomas

Later as I thought about my son's generosity to an undeserving bum, my thoughts turned to a similar situation Jesus faced in the slums of Samaria. Remember the woman at the well? Christ respected her inherent worth and dignity simply because she was a person—a creation of God. Even though she was not following Christ's teachings at that point, there was still a level of respect. We tend to respect people if they believe the way we do and do what we want them to do, but we don't respect them if they don't accept our values. But that's not what Jesus taught. He didn't call us to judge people either. We must allow people to be who they are and try to meet their needs.

Every day on his way to school, Jason passes a man carrying a hand-lettered sign: "Will work for food." Others solicit money from drivers waiting at the traffic light. Jason said, "I realize some will not use the money wisely, but it just doesn't feel right to ignore them or be rude. Sometimes I give my spare change. But not all my experiences are pleasant."

One morning a shabby woman stuck her hand into the open window of his car, stretching toward money she spotted on the console. "I want that dollar!" she insisted. Jason said, "There I was nose to nose with a foul-smelling woman who demanded my lunch money. I handed over the dollar, but I wasn't a cheerful giver that day."

As we face the numerous opportunities to give and deal with the problems that come alongside, we need to remember that God will provide direction. He doesn't intend for his will to be mysterious or hard to understand. He wants us to know what to do. (Which may be something as simple as keeping our windows closed in a crowded intersection!) Our challenge is to listen well and to obey. As God speaks to our hearts, he won't provide an easy-to-follow rule of thumb that applies to every situation. But, one step at a time, one person at a time, we can let his peace rule (be the decider or referee) in our hearts.[6] How comforting to know we all have a personal financial advisor walking with us through the complications of life, providing inspiration, clarity, and peace as we make spiritually informed decisions. In addition, God promises that as we grow in faith we won't be easily deceived "by the cunning and craftiness of men in their deceitful scheming" (Eph. 4:14).

Such was the experience of my friend Marge. The family living behind her was obviously needy. She had observed a bedraggled housewife pinning laundry on a clothesline and two little girls in tattered dresses playing in the dirt. Marge felt compassion and prayed about their physical and spiritual needs. One morning she met the man of the house. He stumbled toward the fence and asked, "Ma'am, could you lend me a couple of bucks for food?"

Later Marge said, "The first question that popped into my mind was, *does he really want food?* But instead of reacting, I told him to wait as I headed inside to seek God's wisdom. Should I give to someone who might use the money foolishly? Perhaps spending it on something harmful like alcohol? Was this encounter an answer to my prayers? Soon a thought came clearly: *I didn't have to determine whether or not my neighbor deserved the money, I only needed to know God's will on that particular occasion.* I felt led to give him two dollars."

Afterward, whenever her neighbor asked for a handout, Marge talked to God about it—sometimes sending up rocket prayers and getting quick answers; at other times pulling aside, waiting on God until peace prevailed. Sometimes Marge gave money to the man, but usually she didn't. She gave the girls new shoes, their mother a dress, and occasionally shared a casserole or homemade bread. Her acts of benevolence eventually reaped spiritual benefits.

One day the man said, "You're the kindest woman I've ever known. Why do you care?" Marge seized the opportunity to share the greatest Gift—her faith in Jesus Christ. Later Marge grinned as she quipped, "Sometimes it's right to give when it isn't logical."

In *Your Finances in Changing Times*, author Larry Burkett agrees. "Many decisions we make in our Christian lives—perhaps even most—do not make sense to the world. Therefore, we make them because of a commitment to God's Word—in other words, out of obedience."[7]

---

*G*iving frees us from the familiar territory of our own needs by opening our mind to the unexplained worlds occupied by the needs of others.

Barbara Bush

Sometimes God asks us to give something even more beneficial than money. We're actually told to demonstrate our love by giving two ways, "with actions and in truth" (1 John 3:18)—not just doing good deeds, but sharing the truths of Christ, exposing false beliefs. Unfortunately, most of us would rather give a little money to God's work than get personally involved. Not surprising when we consider the high cost of such involvement. Loving "in truth" may mean teaching job skills or money management, confronting sinful behavior, role-modeling our values.

When it comes to serving the poor, it seems to me the more appropriate response is *not* giving money. Look at how our government throws money at people, trying to get rid of the problem. Nevertheless, as poverty grows in our world, our attitude toward personal responsibility may need to be reexamined.

A few university students became personally involved with the homeless when they began meeting on Sunday mornings with a group playfully dubbed "The Church under the Bridge." Week after week, the students served donuts and coffee to those gathered under the overpass. But first, they had to listen to the preacher! "The experience was eye-opening," one student claimed. "You really start to care about people when you've been to 'church' with them. These were real people with real needs, but I'm not sure if our small gifts made much of a difference. At least they had warm tummys and, hopefully, warmer hearts when we met with them."

I can't help but believe that those students pleased God with their hands-on ministry, especially when I think about how Jesus identified with the needy. Remember what he said? "Whatever you did for one of the least of these brothers of mine, you did for me" (Matt. 25:40). He considered the smallest deed of charity done for one down-and-out person an act of kindness toward himself.

Of course he did!

Think of it. Jesus, the one who created the world and all its wealth, leaving the splendor of heaven, choosing to live in the mess of struggling humanity as poorest of the poor. Not that Jesus didn't work! For one thing, he labored as a carpenter. But as he traveled from place to place serving others, pleasing God, he was often penniless (or rather denarius-less). Imagine Jesus opening his hand to receive a few coins from the purse of Salome or nibbling a crust of bread offered by one of the other women who followed him.[8]

Visualize King Jesus sleeping on a cot at Lazarus's house, feeling the scratch of handmade woolen blankets. See the Creator of water accepting a cup of cool, refreshing liquid from the hand of Martha, or allowing Mary to fill a basin and wash his feet. Can you imagine the humility, the grace required for the God-man to receive those gifts? No wonder our Lord, the poor, homeless, tired, hungry Jesus, told his disciples, "Anyone who gives you a cup of water in my name . . . will certainly not lose his reward" (Mark 9:41).

On numerous occasions, our son Jason gave his equivalent of a "cup of water" to an indigent man who frequented the dumpster near his apartment. And his benevolence provided many an anecdote and a few important life lessons for all of us. One evening, Jason watched the man poke through the garbage with his stick, retrieving aluminum cans and other "valuables." Feeling compassionate, he fetched a bag of empty drink cans from his kitchen and delivered them personally with the comment, "I'll hang my empties on the dumpster's corner from now on." A big toothless grin from the recipient confirmed the deal.

In the following weeks, the homeless man checked the garbage bin regularly as Jason kept his promise. Occasionally the two exchanged awkward greetings. One night Jason cleaned his kitchen, gathered a bag of trash, dashed outside, and tossed it in the dumpster. A muffled howl emanated from its dark interior. "Ouch! Watch out, man!"

"I couldn't help laughing as I darted back inside," Jason said later. "A peculiar bond had developed between me and the dumpster diver. I felt sort of responsible for him, watched his comings and goings, and from that day on tried not to dump garbage on his head." Jason admitted his "donations" may not have changed the man's life dramatically. Still, just showing a bit of respect seemed the right thing to do.

When we think of demonstrating unconditional love, measuring our lives by the Golden Rule, we can't help but declare, "I can't! Who can?" On the other hand, we know that when God calls us to such impossible heights, he also provides a guide rope to hold us steady as we stumble upward.

Jesus said, "If you love those who love you, what credit is that to you? Even 'sinners' love those who love them. And if you do good to those who are good to you, what credit is that to you? Even 'sinners' do that. And if you lend to those from whom you expect repayment, what credit is that to you? Even 'sinners' lend to 'sinners,' expecting to be repaid in full" (Luke 6:32–34).

An amazing insight turned my thoughts right-side up when I discovered that the word "credit" can also be translated "grace." These verses would then read, "If you love those who love you, what *grace* is that? If you do good to those who are good to you, what *grace* is that? If you lend to those from whom you expect repayment, what *grace* is that to you? Even sinners do that!" Such thinking makes me want to stand up and shout, "Okay, I get it!"

I need basketfuls of grace to give in ways that please God. And, when I give "grace-fully"—when grace inspires me—the issue will never be who gets the "credit."

_R_ight-Side Up

1. When you give, are you motivated by a genuine
   love and respect for the individual? Read the following verses from Proverbs and consider these
   questions: Why does poverty happen? Do you
   think a Christian should give to people who live
   irresponsible lives?
   • Proverbs 20:4, 13
   • Proverbs 23:21
   • Proverbs 28:19–20

2. Read Luke 12:48. Discuss the claim that "from
   everyone who has been given much, much will be
   demanded."

3. Mark 12:41–44 tells the story of a widow's small offering. Why do you think her gift was more than all
   the others?

4. Read the promise of Luke 16:11–12. What are the
   "true riches" you desire?

5. Romans 15:26–27 and 1 Corinthians 4:1–2 help us
   understand our responsibility to share both material and spiritual blessings. What is the message
   of these two passages?

6. What part does grace play as we consider giving to others? What is the message of Ephesians 4:7? Do you give out of a sense of obligation or freedom?

7. Centuries ago the people of Corinth set a good example and established a well-thought-out, spiritually motivated philosophy of giving. Their model with the clear instruction given by Paul is a good one for women like you and me to follow. As you read the following words from *The Message*, consider these questions: What is your philosophy of giving? How will you handle the "plain meaning of the Message of Christ"?

> Remember: A stingy planter gets a stingy crop; a lavish planter gets a lavish crop. I want each of you to take plenty of time to think it over, and make up your own mind what you will give. That will protect you against sob stories and arm-twisting. God loves it when the giver delights in the giving.
>
> God can pour on the blessings in astonishing ways so that you're ready for anything and everything, more than just ready to do what needs to be done. As one psalmist puts it,
>
> > He throws caution to the winds,
> >   giving to the needy in reckless abandon.
> > His right-living, right-giving ways
> >   never run out, never wear out.
>
> This most generous God who gives seed to the farmer that becomes bread for your meals is more than extravagant with you. He gives you something you can then give away, which grows into full-formed lives,

robust in God, wealthy in every way, so that you can be generous in every way, producing with us great praise to God.

Carrying out this social relief work involves far more than helping meet the bare needs of poor Christians. It also produces abundant and bountiful thanksgivings to God. This relief offering is a prod to live at your very best, showing your gratitude to God by being openly obedient to the plain meaning of the Message of Christ. You show your gratitude through your generous offerings to your needy brothers and sisters, and really toward everyone. Meanwhile, moved by the extravagance of God in your lives, they'll respond by praying for you in passionate intercession for whatever you need. Thank God for this gift, his gift. No language can praise it enough!

2 Corinthians 9:6–15

5

When the Going Gets Tough, the Tough . . . Rest

Overcoming Burnout

Come to me, all you who are weary and burdened, and I will give you rest. Take my yoke upon you and learn from me. . . . For my yoke is easy and my burden is light.

Matthew 11:28–30

Back in the sixties, experts on time management claimed that within twenty years advances in technology would radically alter our lives. For one thing, they predicted the soon-to-be-realized advancements would change how many hours a week people worked. The most conservative analysts claimed we'd all enjoy a four-day workweek. More freethinking groups forecasted the average American would work much less than that—a measly twenty-two hours a week. "The great challenge," the pundits said, "would be figuring out what to do with all the excess time."

My hubby, an overworked engineer with IBM, and I got excited and bought a boat. We figured we'd get an early start at doing leisure.

A few years later, we visited our boat in dry dock at a nearby marina and decided to post a For Sale sign on the craft's dusty windshield. Today, decades later, we've seen major advances in technology, but like most of you, we are *not* sitting around eating bonbons, wondering what to do with all the excess time on our hands! Instead, we are running around, doing three things at a time, pecking our next appointments into a PDA with that little pointy thing, or phoning ahead on our cell phones to reschedule a meeting at our next stop. Seems we can't even visit a coffee shop without opening our laptops and checking our email.

No wonder Jesus's promise, "I will give you rest," is so appealing.

Ahhh, sweet rest!

I picture myself with my feet propped up on the railing of the porch or the deck of a cabin cruiser (sigh) as I gaze upon a buttery yellow sunset on the horizon. What is your concept of rest? Whatever comes to mind as you think about it, it probably is *not* the way Jesus sees it. For he no sooner invites us to put aside our multitasking than he asks us to take on another burden—a yoke. Even a city slicker like me knows that donning a yoke means there's work to do. It's not an object associated even loosely with putting one's feet up. Besides that, the only yoke I've ever seen was carved from a huge piece of wood, which makes the contraption neither "easy" nor "light." Obviously there's more in the aforementioned verse of Scripture than first meets the eye. So what did Jesus mean? What is he asking us to do?

A measure of clarity came to my befuddled mind when I looked up some pertinent info. A yoke, it seems, is used to bind two animals together to accomplish a singular task. Usually one of the animals is more mature and skilled in plowing fields and making straight furrows. He is the "lead" animal. The other is younger, thus adding to the equation an extra measure of strength, resilience, and spontaneity. The two yoked together make a perfect team—one providing what is lacking in the other, the two supporting each other with different yet complementary strengths. Even I can understand how that kind of teamwork would not only increase efficiency but also lighten the workload. What a great concept for the farmer! What a good idea for busy women like you and me. Especially when we realize whose yoke we'll be wearing.

Jesus invites us to wear *his* yoke, so it must be perfectly designed to fit our shoulders just right. Think of it. Yoked together with Jesus as we till the rocky soil of human existence! Think about him, the one who created all the fields of the earth, fully knowing the path with its every pitfall and stony place, willingly taking the lead, pulling the weight, setting the pace, making the necessary adjustments. And when I stumble or make a wrong turn, he lifts me up and steers me onto the right path. My task is much simpler than that of the Leader. I must simply trust his leadership and keep in step—one step at a time.

The Upside-Down Truth...

Rest: Not fretting about what might be, but celebrating what already is.

Such a plan simplifies the whole concept of Christian service, taking obedience to a higher level. No longer would women like you and me find ourselves fretting over what we should do and how we should do it. If we would simply accept the yoke, resist the impulse to pull against or wiggle free of the restraints, then it would rest easy on our necks, never binding, chafing, or feeling heavy. When we rest in Jesus, even though we are working—maybe even working really hard—the stress is gone. And stress-free work is restful, productive work. The rows get plowed, the crops are planted, and the harvest grows with minimum effort and lots of satisfaction for both members of the team. It would also solve the puzzle of knowing what God's will might be in a given situation. Being the follower is liberating, freeing us to simply relax and enjoy a close relationship with the One in charge.

God invites you to join **Him** where
He is already at work.

Henry Blackaby

I read somewhere that a good farmer only works his oxen team six hours a day. If that's so, then the seventh hour would begin a period of rest. If only we would follow the example of the good farmer instead of pushing ourselves 24/7! This is more than a good plan. From the beginning of time, God moved to the same rhythm of work and rest. Remember the creation story? In six days God created heaven and earth and everything in it.[1] On the seventh day, he rested.[2]

God's rest was so much more than what we mortals experience when we take a break. It was a time of spiritual contemplation: "God saw all that He had made, and behold, it was very good"(Gen. 1:31 NASB). It was also a time of fellowship. When reading the account, you can't help but notice the use of the plural pronoun "us" (v. 26). Even the name for God, *Elohim*, is in the plural form. I can only imagine the pleasure the Triune God must have felt while celebrating creation—Father, Son, and Holy Spirit accompanied by a watching party of angels,[3] admiring the finished work, rejoicing that it was "very good." In today's vernacular it must have been "totally awesome!" And the holiday observed on the seventh day must have been just as perfect as the work accomplished on the other six.

Thousands of years later God instructed Moses to write the Sabbath principle into law. "Remember the Sabbath day" (Exod. 20:8). Our Father knew we needed to be told in no uncertain terms how life works best, so he spelled it out clearly—work six days, rest the seventh. Isn't it interesting that as the commandments were recorded, most of them beginning "thou shall" or "thou shall not," this one begins with the word "remember"? It's almost as if our heavenly Father looked right into the twenty-first century, got a glimpse of us scurrying around town in our SUVs, and decided to change the tone of that particular command. He knew today's Christian woman would *not* be trying to figure out what to do with all our excess time. He knew we'd be so busy we would forget to take care of ourselves. We'd need to "remember" the importance of rest. Since women are the multitasking champions of the world, it is a message especially pertinent to us.

I must admit I'm as guilty as the next person when it comes to overdoing it. Some days I jump out of bed, grab my purse, and head for the car without pausing for even one spiritual thought. This is not the norm for me, but occasionally I get caught up in the moment and I just forget. And when I begin my day in such a haphazard manner, it usually ends up in total chaos.

One morning, for example, I jumped in my car and sped toward Barnes and Noble, my mind set on buying the latest Elizabeth Berg novel. As I zipped across the parking lot at a faster-than-usual pace, I saw three other cars on a collision course with mine. We screeched to a stop at an unmarked intersection. My heart skipped a beat when I realized all four of us were talking on cell phones, our minds carelessly floating about in cyberspace. Yikes! I yelled to my sister who was listening to the commotion from the other end of my cellular signal, "Lois! I've gotta go. Somebody's got to pay attention." I heard her sigh as I pushed the OFF button.

I know I am not alone in this penchant for moving too fast, doing too much, and not taking enough time off. I know this for sure because I speak to women's groups all the time and some of the ladies confess to it. At a recent retreat I asked the women to take the following fill-in-the-blanks test. I wish you could have heard them hollering out their answers to my quiz. If you are so inclined, you can yell out your answers right now. Believe me, a hearty response will definitely make you feel better, and as an aside, if there's anybody in hearing range, they just might think twice about asking you to take on another project.

The Busy Woman's Fill-in-the-Blanks Test

I'm ready to throw in the . . .
I'm at the end of my . . .
My life is falling . . .
I'm at my wit's . . .
I feel like resigning from the human . . .

We all know the answers because we're all experiencing the same rat race. Just when we think we're getting ahead, along come faster rats. Thankfully, into the rat race comes the invitation of our Lord: "Come to me."

It's an invitation that's been offered to struggling women from the beginning of time. The first came from the lips of God when he called Noah, his wife, and other family members to enter the ark before the rains began.[4] In case you've ever wondered, it is also how Noah collected all those animal pairs to come on board. He didn't go out and round them up; God simply told them to come and they did.[5] Of course God was working on those animals from the inside out, inspiring them to obey. Wouldn't it have been fun to watch that parade? When I think about the animals responding to the call of God without hesitation, following the plan perfectly, I feel embarrassed by the hardness of the human heart. I want to bow before our gracious God and apologize. "I'm sorry we are not more animal-like, less busy with urgent matters, more willing to step in time with our Creator." And when I think about my own crazy behavior, believe me, there are times when I would gladly trade places with, oh, maybe an energetic young ox!

"Come" is the invitation issued by Jesus again and again. "I am the bread of life," he claimed. "He who comes to me will never go hungry" (John 6:35). On another occasion, he said, "If anyone is thirsty, let him come to me and drink" (John 7:37). The Song of Solomon in its simplest form is an invitation for the bride of Christ to come to Jesus and have all her longings for love and intimacy fulfilled in him. One of the final scenes in human history portrays "the Spirit and the bride" saying, "Come!" (Rev. 22:17). The call "come to Me" that has echoed through the ages still reverberates today and is picked up by human hearts in tune with God.

I love how Oswald Chambers expresses this call: "At the most unexpected moments in your life there is this whisper of the Lord—'Come to Me,' and you are immediately drawn to Him. Personal contact with Jesus changes everything."[6] Jesus promises to relieve our burdens, but only if we will come to him. Please note the invitation is to come not to a representative of him—a counselor or friend, not to some substitute god, not even to what he says. Come to Jesus himself! God the Father went to great lengths, including the sacrifice of his Son on the cross, to open up the way for us to "come boldly to the throne of grace" (Heb. 4:16 NKJV).

"Come to me, all you who are weary and burdened, and I will give you rest" (Matt. 11:28)—this is perhaps the most appealing invitation of all. A different translation reads, "Come to me, all who are tired from carrying heavy loads" (GNT). Another version invites "all whose work is hard" (NEB). Most of us have no trouble admitting we are carrying a heavy load, and most of us can say our work is hard. Pressure, conflicts, troubled relationships, and unresolved personal issues are weighing many of us down. At least half of today's marriages end in divorce, and many young mothers are parenting alone, usually while holding down a full-time job. There are over twenty million grandmothers in our country, and more than four million of them are primary caregivers for their grandkids.[7] On top of everything else, many women are taking care of their aging parents. Now that's hard work! No wonder Jesus said, "Come with me by yourselves to a quiet place and get some rest" (Mark 6:31).

There's so much work to do in this old world, and so few women to do it.

Anonymous

So what would observing the Sabbath look like to today's Christian woman? Perhaps it would include a walk in the park (not to cross "exercise" off your to-do list), spending an unhurried afternoon with a soul mate or prayer partner, reading from the Psalms, studying a passage from Colossians (my personal favorite), looking up word meanings in a Bible dictionary, writing thoughts in a journal, resting in a hammock, reading fiction, romancing your husband. You may think these ideas simplistic, but many of the women I know seldom find time for these things. Work, after-work appointments, carpooling, sports, homework, cooking, cleaning, and church activities leave them little time to cultivate relationships or even nurture their relationship with God.

We long for serenity of soul, peace of mind, and a quiet heart, but rest is elusive. What would it take for us to realize the desire of our heart? The fourth chapter of Hebrews gives us a clue to the promise of rest, but it also warns us that it is possible to miss it altogether. "Therefore, let us fear if, while a promise remains of entering His rest, any one of you may seem to have come short of it" (v. 1 NASB). The chapter also tells us why: "It was not united by faith by those who heard" (v. 2 NASB) and some "failed to enter because of disobedience" (v. 6 NASB). It also reveals what must happen before we can rest: "be diligent to enter that rest" (v. 11 NASB).

Now that's the concept that turns my thoughts upside down. God is offering the gift of rest, then tells us we must "be diligent" to attain it. Another translation says we must "make every effort" to receive it (NIV). The King James Version uses the word "labor." Sounds like rest involves hard work. Does that make sense to you? What kind of effort does God require? Must we work at not working?

I find it interesting that immediately following Jesus's command to "be diligent to enter that rest" is a thought-provoking description of the Word of God. Seems to me the answer is found in these words: "For the word of God is living and active and sharper than any two-edged sword, and piercing as far as the division of soul and spirit, of both joints and marrow, and able to judge the thoughts and intentions of the heart" (Heb. 4:12 NASB). Seems to me the work required is being diligent, making every effort to put ourselves in a place where the Word of God can have an effect on us. This doesn't mean simply signing up for a Bible study group—not even a Precept course. It means allowing ourselves to be exposed to the truth. It may include hearing, reading, studying, memorizing, and meditating, but not as a discipline, not for acquiring more insight or accumulating facts, but so that we may know God and understand ourselves.

Look at how God's Word is described. It is "alive" and "active"—having divine life, being full of spiritual energy. Because it is a living thing, it has a life-giving and life-changing effect on us.[8] Like standing under the showerhead so warm water can wash over our bodies, being under the influence of truth cleanses the thoughts and intentions of our heart. When I put myself in a place where I can benefit from God's Word, change happens. I begin to understand why I react the way I do, why I want to be in control, or why I can't let go of certain problems, situations, or people. I

If you want rest, you must work to obtain it.

The Upside-Down Truth . . .

figure out why I function (and dysfunction) the way I do. I see areas where I need to grow. With this kind of insight comes a great sense of peace . . . and rest.

The Word of God is also "sharp" like a sword. It helps me cut through the superfluous, corrects my course, points out new directions. Daily interaction with truth changes my perspective. I'm able to discern between things that are good and things that are better or best. This helps me eliminate urgent, time-consuming, or self-serving activity and concentrate on what's most important—the plans God has for me. It also makes a piercing distinction between two parts of my being that seem very similar. I start to see the difference between ideas and solutions that come from my own psyche or "soul"—my mind, will, emotions, and personality, including my unmet needs, unfilled longings, unrealized dreams—and things that come from my "spirit"—the place where God dwells in me, that part of me that wants only what he wants. Truth helps me discern between thoughts and feelings that come from just me and impressions that come from God.

When I am open and honest about myself before God, I move through the complicated maze of human emotions into the light and freedom of truth.[9] I am able to enter into his rest—rest in who I am, rest in relationship with others, rest in my place in society, rest in what I choose to do, rest while using my spiritual gifts and desires to serve God.

So, if rest is work and the work we do for God is really just a matter of resting in him, I wonder what a day in the life of Jesus's follower would be like. Probably similar to one described in the Gospel of Mark.

Jesus showed us firsthand how to serve God without feeling put-upon or frazzled. First of all, he didn't strike out on his own like we, in our enthusiasm for the mission, sometimes do. Rather, he waited, taking care of his own spiritual self, nurturing his relationship with his Father, and getting clear direction from the Holy Spirit. He didn't budge from the banks of the Jordan River until he received the blessing and power that came when God touched him. Then he set out to do his bidding supercharged by divine energy, ready to do whatever, whenever!

The first stop on his mission tour would be the wilderness. Does that surprise you? Or is it just like what happens to you and me? We think we're prepared to do some special task for God, but before we embark on the journey something unexpected happens, something unexplainable and hard. Later, when we look back on our experience, we realize it was a test of our faith or endurance and an important part of our preparation. Once we've grown through the test or overcome some huge temptation, we are finally ready to follow God's plan.

Jesus, as he set the example for us, was tempted and encountered wild beasts for an excruciating forty days. At the end of the wilderness experience, angels appeared and ministered to him. I can only imagine our Lord dusting himself off, straightening his robes, and drawing strength from his encounter with celestial beings, emerging from the wilderness with new power and determination to continue his mission. Keeping the pace the Father had set for his Son.

And look at what he accomplished in just one day![10]

He preached fearlessly to the Galileans, the very ones who'd recently taken John into custody, asking them to repent and believe in the gospel. Afterward, during a long walk by the Sea of Galilee, he spotted several fishermen, including Simon, Andrew, James, and John, and engaged them in spiritual conversations that changed the direction of their lives. He said, "'Follow Me, and I will make you become fishers of men.' Immediately they left their nets and followed Him" (Mark 1:17–18 NASB).

As evening approached, they went into Capernaum and entered the synagogue to teach. If Jesus felt fatigue, it wasn't obvious to those who heard him speak. They were amazed at his wisdom and authority. He no sooner finished speaking than a man with an unclean spirit was brought to him, and Jesus delivered him of the demon.

When the crowd dispersed, Jesus and the four "fishers of men" went to Simon's house. They were probably looking forward to a bit of rest, but before they could even find a place to sit, Simon introduced Jesus to his mother-in-law, who was sick, her fever soaring out of control. The Scripture says Jesus took her by the hand and as soon as she stood up, she served them.[11] What a miracle! Not only did her fever leave her, but if she followed the customs of the day, she washed their dirty feet and then served tea and cookies. She must have been overjoyed to be able to serve Jesus and his new disciples in this way. And I'm sure they appreciated finally having a few moments of rest and relaxation.

Their R & R was cut short when the neighbors overheard Jesus was in town. Before dark they began bringing sick and demon-possessed friends and relatives to Jesus, asking him to set them free. So many people came that Mark wrote, "The whole city had gathered at [Simon's] door" (Mark 1:33 NASB). Before he went to bed, Jesus healed many of them.

When Jesus retired that night, I think he rested well, knowing he'd followed his Father's lead and accomplished the work planned for him. Regardless of how exhausted he may have been, he did not choose to sleep in the next morning. What he needed was more than physical rest;

he needed spiritual rest. At dawn he found a place to get alone with God, a quiet place to pray.

Spiritually refreshed, he was ready to face another challenging day, speaking, walking long dusty miles, healing, confronting demons. Physically draining work, energized by the power and presence of his Father.

Think back on one of your incredibly busy days. At the end of the day were you able to rest well? Did you feel content?

There's one particular day that will stick in my memory forever. I had packed my bags the day before and awoke before sunrise for an early flight to Rochester, New York. I knew I had to change planes in Chicago and allowed an hour to make it from one gate to another.

My plane departed on schedule from Dallas–Fort Worth, giving me enough time to settle in my seat for a nap. But I'd no sooner asked for a pillow and blankie than the man seated next to me began to talk. I stifled a yawn when I noticed tears pooling in his eyes. Then he launched into a detailed story about his twenty-four-year-old son, a guy who'd just lost his battle with drug addiction. The grief-stricken daddy was on his way home from the funeral. I breathed a quick prayer: "Lord, this is a divine appointment. Give me the right words to say. Help me listen well." So, I skipped my nap and listened—for more than two hours!

When we arrived in Chicago, as amazing as it may seem, I was completely at rest and full of God's peace. I literally bounced through the terminal toward the assigned gate. Then I discovered the second leg of my journey would be delayed four hours. I grabbed some lunch and called the event coordinator in Rochester. As I sat in the terminal watching the crew outside de-icing the planes, I felt a knot tighten in my stomach. I'd never flown during an ice storm, and I wasn't sure I wanted to! "Lord, I'm not in control here," I whispered as I fumbled through my carry-on bag, looking for a book. "You know how much I like to feel that I am in charge," I continued, "but I know you, the Great Controller of Every Circumstance, are with me. Help me trust you." As I opened my book and started to read, I thought, *How long has it been since I've had four hours to read?* This was turning out to be a very good day!

I finally boarded the plane five (not four) hours behind schedule, and arrived at the church in Rochester with just enough time for a sound check before it was time to speak to a large group of women. I felt a burst of energy as I mounted the platform.

After speaking, I got involved in several conversations and signed a few books before I was able to check into my hotel. Once there it felt good to take off the clothes I'd been wearing for eighteen hours, slip into my comfy pajamas, and crawl into bed. Before I switched off the lights, I felt a point of identity with Jesus. I set the alarm for 6:00 a.m. (5:00 a.m. Texas time!).

I knew I needed to be up early to pray, read over my notes, and refresh myself with the text I'd be teaching the next day. I wouldn't dare try to serve the women who'd come to the retreat without knowing God was with me, leading me, filling me with his power and presence, giving me inner strength.

Did I rest well after I turned off the lights? Yes, of course I did! It was not simply physical rest but soul rest, that deep-seated contentment that comes from knowing I'd served my Father well.

Ahh, sweet rest!

*R*ight-Side Up

1. Read Isaiah 26:3. What is the promise? What are the conditions you and I must meet to receive the promise? Define the word "stayed."

2. Proverbs 19:23 claims that rest comes when we understand the fear of the Lord. Does that concept seem confusing to you? What does it mean to "fear" God? Use a concordance and give supporting Scripture to back up your conclusions.

3. What is the prescription for rest given in Psalm 91:1–2? Compare the verse from another translation: "You who sit down in the High God's presence, spend the night in Shaddai's shadow, say this: 'God, you're my refuge! I trust in you and I am safe'" (Message). Discuss this concept.

4. The Old Testament prophet Jeremiah wrote the following words about rest: "This is what the LORD says: 'Stand at the crossroads and look; ask for the ancient paths, ask where the good way is, and walk in it, and you will find rest for your souls'" (6:16). Does this sound like a life of leisure or labor? What was the response of those who heard Jeremiah's words? Why do you think they responded this way?

5. Hebrews 4 teaches us that it is possible to "come short of" the rest Jesus promises (v. 1 NASB). It also tells us to "labor" or "hasten" or "be diligent" to enter into that rest. Does that concept seem upside down to you? Why or why not? What kind of rest is this chapter talking about? Discuss the part that faith and obedience play in understanding and experiencing God's rest.

6. Acts 15:5–11 describes a controversy that arose in the early church. These verses discuss a "yoke" that doesn't fit well—following rules and religious systems in order to be accepted by the religious leaders of that day. Is this a problem today? Is it a problem for you?

7. There are three imperatives in Matthew 11:28–30, three things we must do in order to find rest: "Come . . . take . . . learn." To whom are we to come? What are we to take? What do we need to learn?

6

Definitely Flawed,
Yet Deeply Loved

Facing Insecurities and Fears

God demonstrates his own love for us in this: While we
were still sinners, Christ died for us.

Romans 5:8

Sometimes I find myself thinking like many other Christian women, *If only I were good enough, smart enough, pretty
enough, or thin enough . . . then God would really love me! Maybe
then I would be able to please God.* When my thoughts turn
to spiritual matters I feel even more unacceptable. I am
hopelessly damaged by sin. I'm tempted by the craziest
things and have made a gazillion wrong choices. Some
days I don't have a clue what God wants me to do. So

how could I, mess that I am, be accepted—and loved—by a perfect, holy God?

The truth is, God delights in loving the unlovely, the flawed, and the broken. God loved us enough to send his Son to die on the cross in our place. I am a woman worth saving. And so are you! He is pleased with us simply because we believe in him. He is our Abba, our heavenly daddy, and we are his daughters, warts and all!

Don't you find it interesting how music expresses the feelings and the confusion that most of us feel? How many songs have been written about love? Songs that describe the way we feel or ask the questions most of us have about this hard-to-understand emotion? It's usually the country songs that say it best. Their down-to-earth lyrics crooned with a Texas twang accompanied by a steel guitar . . . well, they just strum the ole heartstrings. Country music gets to the heart of the matter, literally, addressing the thangs (oops, I meant "things") that are dearest to a Texan's life—like our trucks, our dogs, our cowboy friends, and the feelings that tie it all together.

So sometimes, especially when I'm feeling blue, I turn off the classical and go country. Have you ever heard "You Broke My Heart and Stomped That Sucker Flat"? How about "I've Got Tears in My Ears from Lyin' on My Back and Cryin' Over You"?[1] Now I ask you, are there words better than those to express that lousy feeling? I don't think so! And lest you think we Texans wallow about in melancholy moods all the time, on our better days you'll hear someone singing "Take Me to the Corn Field Honey and I'll Kiss You Between the Ears."

Okay, enough!

I'm sure you get the picture. Is there a classical love song recorded that comes close to telling it like it really is?

One of my personal favorites when it comes to songs-with-a-twang is "I Want to Know What Love Is." It doesn't provide any solutions, but at least it poses the question; it makes me think. (Thanks, Wynonna!) Frankly, many of the women I know are not only frustrated, they're downright confused—even more confused than I am. Their needs are not being met in their guy-girl relationships because they don't know what real love is.

What is love, anyway?

Several years ago, a friend I'll call Jennifer shared some of her insight into the subject. "My husband is the love of my life," she told me. "I married my soul mate." She sighed deeply and continued. "I enjoy the way he rubs my back before we say good night and go to sleep. Well, sometimes we don't just roll over and go to sleep, if you get my drift."

Fast-forward a few years. Jennifer's husband finally found the courage to say something he'd been holding in way too long. He confessed that he didn't like to rub Jen's back. Not anymore. Not at all!

Jennifer was crushed. Not that she couldn't do without the rubdown. It was just, well, she thought *he* liked it. Her mind replayed the things he'd said, the playful routine, the lovemaking, the cozy afterglow. The more she thought about it, the more hurt she felt. Had he been making things up, faking his feelings? Was he rubbing her back because he felt obligated or, even worse, for what he might get out of it? The thought that she'd been manipulated and deceived eventually led them to seek counseling.

If you are thinking Jennifer was making a big deal out of nothing, think about how you'd feel. There's not a woman among us who wants to be teased. We all want every word, every touch, every look to be authentic. We long for passion that's real, men who are absolutely gaga over us. Is that too much to ask?

In the counselor's office, Jennifer put all her thoughts on the table. *Her husband didn't love her. Love doesn't pretend or play around with a woman's emotions.* And the way he kept quiet about his "real" feelings, that was tantamount to a big fat lie.

Her husband thought the opposite. "Love is doing, not feeling," he said. "When I gave back rubs, it was just that, a gift. In my opinion, that is the highest expression of love." As far as his feelings were concerned, he had felt real joy in serving his wife in ways that pleased and comforted her. He'd just grown tired of back rubbing. Simple as that!

Jennifer needed some time to think. After a few days of soul searching, she came to an "Aha!" moment—a spiritual epiphany. She understood a truth she'd heard many times, one that in her mind had become nothing more than a cliché. *Love is not a feeling; love is a choice.* I'm glad to report that Jen and "the love of her life" survived the crisis and their marriage became even more intimate, more "real."

Our Abba knew we'd want to know what love is, so he inspired a comprehensive description of it in the New Testament. His definition may seem upside down to most of us. But written in the everyday language of *The Message*, it's easier for most of us to grasp. Why, it almost sounds Texan.

Love is not something you feel; love is something you choose to do.

Love never gives up.
Love cares more for others than for self.
Love doesn't want what it doesn't have.
Love doesn't strut,
Doesn't have a swelled head,
Doesn't force itself on others,
Isn't always "me first,"
Doesn't fly off the handle,
Doesn't keep score of the sins of others,
Doesn't revel when others grovel,
Takes pleasure in the flowering of truth,
Puts up with anything,
Trusts God always,
Always looks for the best,
Never looks back,
But keeps going to the end.

1 Corinthians 13:4–7 Message

While we women may be sharp enough to understand the words, I'm wondering if we're spiritual enough to really get a handle on what it all means. It's a complicated issue. "The two most difficult things to get straight in life are love and God," Eugene Peterson claims. "More often than not, the mess people make of their lives can be traced to failure or stupidity or meanness in one or both of these areas."[2] Pretty bold statement, isn't it? But there's something about it that strikes a chord with me—and I don't mean a chord on a steel guitar!

Have any of us ever loved one single person with that kind of love? We have probably managed to get it right on a few counts, but failed miserably on others. We may have been successful in controlling our anger a few times and can honestly say, "I didn't keep score," not that time. Or we may be able to claim, "I haven't given up," at least not yet. But on other points, like "puts up with anything" or "trusts God always," we have to admit total failure. Is it even possible to love another person like that as long as we live here on planet Earth? Still most of us would say, "I'd like to meet those standards. I'm trying."

---

*W*e love, because He first loved us.
The Apostle John

Have you ever been loved that much? Some of us could say we've been loved well by someone very special—a doting father, an adoring husband, or a close friend. Unfortunately many cannot make that claim. One in four women in our society have been sexually abused (some by their own daddy). Half of America's marriages end in divorce. Many women who stay married are divorced emotionally, separated from their husbands by some secret sin or emotional problem. Many of the women I know long to be loved. Some of them are lonely, sad, and depressed. Most of them know that Jesus loves them, but to be honest, they have a hard time saying their relationship with him completely fills the emptiness inside. You may be thinking, *I know Jesus loves me.* If you don't know it for sure, let me reassure you. He really does!

Love can wait to give; lust can't wait to get.

All of us women are flawed. Most of us have been deeply hurt. That kind of reality is hard to accept, much less embrace in ways that make you *feel* as

The Upside-Down Truth...

loved as you actually are. If you have never been loved unconditionally by another human being, is it really enough knowing you are loved by Jesus? Are the arms of Jesus adequate when you long to be hugged by "real" arms, arms that are attached to a strong, sensitive man? Do the "kisses of his mouth"[3] really satisfy your love hunger? Is Jesus sufficient when you want somebody to talk to, somebody who'll go a bit deeper than "news, weather, and sports" or his latest insights from *Gilligan's Island* reruns? Is it possible for Jesus to be your best, or maybe only, friend, lover, confidant?

One woman who lived ages ago found him to be all that and more. When she met him, she'd already tried all the love-hunger solutions the world has to offer. She'd been married five times and was living with candidate number six. I wonder what would cause a woman to take the matrimonial plunge that many times. Perhaps she simply needed someone to take care of her. It was extremely hard in that culture for a woman to make ends meet without a husband. (Not so different from our society today, huh?) Maybe she just couldn't bear the thought of being alone. It could have been she was trying to fill the God-shaped vacuum in her heart with some human substitute for God. Whatever the reason, everything changed when she found out how much Jesus loved her.

As the story goes, Jesus and a group of disciples left Judea in the midst of a controversy and headed toward Galilee. The Bible says they had to pass through Samaria. Actually there were three routes they could have taken, so the visit to Samaria was a choice Jesus made—a choice for a specific purpose. When the men reached the village of Sychar, Jesus sat down by the well of Jacob to rest, and his disciples went into town to buy something to eat.

While he waited, a woman balancing a water pot on her head sauntered up the pathway, heading toward the well. When she spotted Jesus, her heart must have skipped a beat as she sucked in a big gulp of air. At this time of day she hadn't expected to see anyone, especially not a man. *Who is that? Why is he here?*

Jesus spoke quickly, perhaps hoping to calm her fears. "Will you give me a drink?" (John 4:7).

I wonder what the woman felt when this handsome, compassionate stranger asked her for a drink of water. Talk about conflicting emotions! She knew that most Jews held a low opinion of Samaritans. Yet she must have been fascinated by him, drawn to him. His gentleness, the kindness she noticed in his eyes, were qualities she may have never seen in another man.

"You are a Jew and I am a Samaritan woman," she began. "How can you ask me for a drink?" (v. 9). She shifted and continued, "Jews have no dealings with Samaritans."[4] But we know that they did deal with them on a certain level. The disciples had just gone shopping into the village. The truth is, Jews didn't mind doing business with the Samaritans; they just wouldn't drink after them. Prejudices ran deep in that area, sort of like they did in the Deep South following the Civil War. Some people still hold on to these kinds of prejudices today.

Whatever the woman was feeling, Jesus knew. He continued quickly, "If you knew the gift of God and who it is that asks you for a drink, you would have asked him and he would have given you living water" (v. 10).

By this time the woman was totally confused. Jesus didn't have a bucket or a jar. And, to make it even more perplexing, now he was offering her water when just ten seconds before he'd asked her for some. "'Sir,' the woman said, 'you have nothing to draw with and the well is deep. Where can you get this living water?'" (v. 11).

Jesus answered, "Everyone who drinks this water will be thirsty again, but whoever drinks the water I give him will never thirst. Indeed, the water I give him will become in him a spring of water welling up to eternal life" (vv. 13–14).

I can imagine the woman pushing aside her questions as she tried to figure out what she was feeling. This was not a physical attraction—she knew what that felt like. No, this was something different, unrecognizable. The emotions came from a deeper place in her, from the very depths of her soul. Gazing at him in breathless wonder, she answered, "Sir, give me this water so that I won't get thirsty and have to keep coming here to draw water" (v. 15).

Do you hear the angst in her request? *So I won't have to come here for water.* I wonder how uncomfortable it had been for her to take care of this simple task day after day. Coming to the well was a social event for the other women. Had the others avoided her, whispered among themselves, refused to make eye contact? Were they intentionally cruel? Verbally abusive? (Believe me, women can be mean-spirited at times!) That must have been what made the woman's daily visit to the well a job to be dreaded.

Interrupting her thoughts, Jesus made another request. "Go, call your husband and come back" (v. 16).

I can't even imagine what the woman must have felt at that moment—did she have an anxiety attack? Was she gripped with fear? Filled with guilt? Confused? Her pulse racing, palms sweating? Finally, she spat out the truth—at least it was true, technically. "I don't have a husband!"

Jesus's eyes must have pierced her very soul as he said, "I know. You don't have a husband right now. But you have had five and the man you are living with now is not your husband" (see vv. 17–18).

The direction the conversation had taken made her uncomfortable. I know this because she quickly changed the subject. (It's a tactic most of us women have perfected for such a time as this.) She asked Jesus a question. But I think she may have been surprised by the deeply spiritual dialogue her simple query opened up. Jesus told her that salvation "is from the Jews" and that he was the Messiah, the Christ. Then he revealed a mind-boggling truth, one that many Christians today still don't understand—that worship has nothing to do with being in a place like Jerusalem, or even in a church, for that matter. It is done in our spirits and based upon truth, not bound by a certain time or place. He told her God was seeking women just like her to worship him that way. I'm sure her heart beat at a faster-than-usual pace as she considered what he was saying—*in spirit, in truth.*

She must have understood, for she left her water pot, forgetting what she'd come to the well to do, gathered up her skirt, and ran back into the village to tell the men what had happened. She had met "the Christ."

The story concludes that "many of the Samaritans from that town believed in him because of the woman's testimony, 'He told me everything I ever did'" (v. 39). The new believers asked Jesus to stay with them, and he stayed there two days. "Many more believed because of His word; and they were saying to the woman, 'It is no longer because of what you said that we believe, for we have heard for ourselves and know that this One is indeed the Savior of the world'" (vv. 41–42 NASB).

What an incredible story! One that not only opens our eyes to the meaning of eternal life but gives us a glimpse of

Jesus's love for women like you and me. Jesus loved the Samaritan woman like she'd never been loved before—unconditionally, completely, everlastingly. And he loves you and me the very same way. What happened at that well proves it. I've listed some of the most convincing evidence:

- *Love always has you in mind.* Love remembers. Jesus knew where this woman was, and he knew she needed him. He'd been thinking about her though miles separated them. Put yourselves into the picture. Sometimes I think about Jesus coming to Grapevine, Texas. He knows where I live and that I need him. When I wake up feeling thirsty (spiritually speaking, that is!) before I can get to the source of water—the Bible on my desk, or "Quick Verse" on my computer—I realize something that takes my breath away. Jesus is already standing there, waiting for me, having decided eons ago that on this particular day, as on every other day of my life, *I must go through Grapevine.*

- *Love finds or creates opportunities to be together.* Jesus said he was going to swing through Samaria, as if it were not a part of his eternal plan. Think about the serendipity moments in your life when Jesus showed up bringing some moment of grace or love. He may have come to you in a blossom or on the wings of a butterfly. He may have been in the hug your grandbaby gave you or in some kindness expressed by a caring friend. Countless times a day, again and again, in unexpected intimate moments he comes to us.

- *Love doesn't mind extending a favor.* And a really good friend feels free to *ask* a favor. "May I have a drink of water?" We come to Jesus all the time asking for his blessings and gifts. But here he is the one asking. It turns my mind upside down to think of him desiring a favor of me. If you were standing face-to-face with Jesus today, what would he ask you to give him? What could you and I possibly present that would bless the Lord? Perhaps a few words of worship? Maybe a song of praise? Could we offer a Mary-of-Bethany anointing of precious oil?[5] Would those gifts be like a refreshing drink of water to him?

- *Love holds no prejudice.* Culture, social position, differences in age, outward appearance, religious traditions, and gender make no difference when love is present. Jesus loved the Samaritan woman even though she didn't know who he was. She didn't know he was worthy of worship, much less *how* to worship him, or where. Jesus knows everything about women like you and me—the good, the bad, and the really bad—but it doesn't change his love for us. We are "accepted in the beloved" (Eph. 1:6 KJV). As incredible as it may seem, he even calls us his beloved. "You are my beloved, you are my friend."[6]

- *Love doesn't minimize a person's feelings.* Jesus doesn't say "don't feel that way" but invites us to talk, pouring out the words just as they are without pretense or excuse. He never asks us to deny our hurts or act like injustices didn't happen. He doesn't expect us to put on a happy face when we feel bad. Instead, he asks all of us to "let your requests be made known" (Phil. 4:6). Because Jesus loves me, I can be real with him. And I feel loved when I can be authentic without fear of rejection or shame.

- *Love listens well and hears what is behind the words.* "The well is too deep," the Samaritan woman said. Jesus saw into her soul and realized the "well" was deeper than she even knew. He thought of the depth of human nature, the deep hurt and problems of human life, and he must have been moved with compassion. Think of the conflict and trouble inside your own heart. Jesus cared about her "deep wells" just as he cares about yours and mine.[7]

- *Love shares the most important issues of life.* Jesus didn't allow the conversation to bob about on the surface. Instead, he used the discussion about water to open up a conversation about eternal matters. He not only promised a drink to quench the woman's immediate thirst but also a spring of life-giving water bubbling up inside. Jesus loves us enough that he gave his life for us so we can live forever in heaven with him.[8] There's no greater evidence of his love than that!

- *Love doesn't criticize or look for an opportunity to preach a sermon.* Love offers grace and forgiveness. Jesus didn't quickly point a finger or make an accusation: *You are a sinful woman.* He talked with her about her failures, her insatiable thirst for love, the gnawing loneliness that led her into five marriages.[9] Then the slate was wiped clean. Her transgressions would never be mentioned again. Jesus doesn't have a critical attitude about any one of his children. He knows all about our faults, weaknesses, temptations, but instead of seeing us as unworthy (as we sometimes see ourselves), he sees us as forgiven and perfectly clean. "Now, you are clean" (John 15:3). What amazing love!

- *Love doesn't focus on past failures but on the future.* The failures in the Samaritan woman's life became the building blocks of her future, giving her a message relevant to women everywhere, at all times. Once she met Jesus, she couldn't stop talking about him—who he was and what he said! Because Jesus loves us, he takes the everyday circumstances of our lives, helps us put them in the right perspective, and shows us how they can be used for our future good. What I consider my biggest failures in life, Jesus sees as opportunities. He shows me how to use my experiences, even the ones I wish I could forget, to help other people.

- *Love sees the best in a person.* Jesus didn't see the Samaritan woman as an adulteress, a social outcast, or an emotional cripple. He saw her, just as he sees you and me, as complete, righteous, and free.[10]

When you were growing up, did you ever sing the children's hymn "Jesus Loves Me"? If you did, you probably did so with lots of gusto and confidence. "Jesus loves me! This I know, for the Bible tells me so." Unfortunately, as we grow up, the message can get a bit blurred by the problems and pain of our complicated lives. Sometimes it takes a conscious effort to remember that simple truth. Jesus loves you! And just in case you're wondering, there is nothing you can do to keep him from loving you. A bad attitude won't stop his love. You can't be too confused or too hurt. You can't have too many problems. You can't be divorced or married too many times to know the unconditional love of our Lord. Nothing, and I do mean nothing, will ever be able to separate you or me from the everlasting love of Jesus. "Neither death, nor life, nor angels, nor principalities, nor things present, nor things to come, nor powers, nor height, nor depth, nor any other created thing, will be able to separate us from the love of God" (Rom. 8:38–39 NASB).

I love the way *The Message* reads:

So, what do you think? With God on our side like this, how can we lose? If God didn't hesitate to put everything on the line for us, embracing our condition and exposing himself to the worst by sending his own Son, is there anything else he wouldn't gladly and freely do for us? And who would dare tangle with God by messing with one of God's chosen? Who would dare even to point a finger? The One who died for us—who was raised to life for us!—is in the presence of God at this very moment sticking up for us. Do you think anyone is going to be able to drive a wedge between us and Christ's love for us? There is no way! Not trouble, not hard times, not hatred, not hunger, not homelessness, not bullying threats, not backstabbing, not even the worst sins listed in Scripture. . . . None of this fazes us because Jesus loves us. I'm absolutely convinced that nothing—nothing living or dead, angelic or demonic, today or tomorrow, high or low, thinkable or unthinkable—absolutely nothing can get between us and God's love because of the way that Jesus our Master has embraced us.

Romans 8:31–39

Ann, a woman I met recently, described her relationship with Jesus—how she has experienced an incredible, undeserved, and totally unexpected love, a love that has held her close and won't let her go. As I listened to Ann, my thoughts turned to the Samaritan woman. Though their circumstances were completely different, their empty lives, their longings to be loved, were the same.

Ann is a twin. When she was growing up, people couldn't keep from making comparisons. "My sister was tall and thin," Ann said, "and I was short and round. Everybody commented about how pretty my sister was, so I concluded that 'tall and thin' equaled pretty and 'short and round' meant ugly. Early on, I decided I'd probably never get married. Nobody would want me."

As soon as Ann graduated from high school, she got a job, and her life became routine. So routine that she began to wonder, *Why would anybody want to grow up when it means you go to work, come home, do your chores, go to bed, get up the next morning, and do it all over again?*

"I was lonely, Gracie," Ann confessed. "My sister had married, and I didn't have any friends."

Since their parents used to drop the twins off at church, Ann had some spiritual background. So she started looking in the Bible for answers. Ann's voice took on an energetic tone as she explained, "One night I was reading in the Psalms, and it just occurred to me that David's purpose in life was his relationship with God. I knelt and asked Jesus to be my purpose for living. I don't know how long I knelt there clinging to the side of my bed, but when I got up I knew that if I never had a friend, if I never married, Jesus was enough. He literally became the love of my life."

Ann joined a church and began teaching a class of teenage girls. One day a young man stopped by the church to pick up his sister. His name was Bob.

Bob and Ann became friends. Ann said, "We liked to be together, but it wasn't really dating. We'd get together and talk. We talked for hours at a time, about everything. Eventually our conversations took on a more serious and personal tone. We began talking about marriage. Neither of us wanted to make a mistake so we tried to cover all the issues. One day, I laughed and told Bob, 'We've talked so much that I wonder, if we do get married, will we be able to find anything to talk about!'"

Eventually, as love would have it, Bob and Ann married. Ann said, "Bob thought I was beautiful, but our love for each other was based on much more than appearance. Bob loved me, my heart, the person I'd become. He called me his

'Sweetie.' I don't want to make it sound like a fairy tale, but we seldom argued and never talked disrespectfully to one another. Our marriage was based upon respect, compassion, and God's unconditional love. We were committed to each other and to God."

Bob and Ann were married twenty-nine years and had two sons.

Ann's voice cracked as she revealed, "After twenty-seven years of marriage, we faced a crisis that tested our faith and our love for each other. Bob was diagnosed with brain cancer. Two weeks later he had surgery and began treatment. The whole ordeal happened so fast. It shocked and saddened us, but we wanted to stay positive. We prayed, 'Lord, we don't know why you have given us this assignment, but we will honor you.'"

After his surgery, Ann asked only one favor from God. "Lord, if Bob just remembers me and if he is still sweet to me, I can do this. Please don't let the cancer change the man I love." Thankfully, when Ann got to visit him in the ICU, his first words were "There's my sweetie."

On another occasion, after a debilitating round of chemo, several nurses were attending Bob. Ann said he could barely hold his body up, was completely bald, and was barely able to speak. "Bob," Ann teased, "look at all these women taking care of you. God has blessed you so much." She smiled and continued, "Bob looked into my face and breathed out the words, 'I choose you.'"

Ann said, "That moment was one of the most intimate of my life. I knew those words came not only from the mouth of my husband but from my spiritual husband, Jesus. 'I choose you.' I had never felt more loved."

After two years of battling cancer, Bob passed away. Of course Ann grieved and felt lonely. But Jesus became even more real and close. He was enough to see her through her grief and loneliness, and he is still enough today.

Recently when we talked about it, Ann said, "I don't understand why God looked down on me and gave me this incredible love. I don't know why God showed me such favor. I don't know why he loves me so much."

I pressed the phone to my ear so I could hear Ann's quivering voice. The words came barely above a whisper. "Gracie, I just don't know. I only hope that somehow I have given back . . ."

Later that evening my mind replayed the phone conversation I'd had with my new friend Ann. And I couldn't help but compare the deep emotion she had expressed with the shallow concepts we hear so much about in the friendship circles of the world.

I closed my eyes and spoke out loud, "Thank you, Jesus, for loving me too."

Right-Side Up

1. Many women followed Jesus and lovingly served him while he took care of people's needs. Read the following. Who were these women, and what did they do to demonstrate their love for him?
   - Mark 15:40–41
   - Luke 7:36–39
   - Luke 8:1–3
   - Mark 14:3
   - Luke 10:38–42
   - Luke 23:55–56; 24:1–10

2. After the resurrection certain women waited in the upper room for the promised Holy Spirit. Discuss what happened in Acts 1:14.

3. Women were active in the early church in a variety of ministries. Who were these two women, and what did they do?
   - Romans 16:1–2
   - Acts 18:1–3; 1 Corinthians 16:19

4. After Pentecost there was no looking back, no longing for the good old days when Jesus was with them physically. Why is this true? What helped them move on? Read John 14:16–18.

5. Read John 14:20. How would the new relationship be different from what the disciples had already experienced?

6. Read John 14:21. Describe the woman who loves Jesus. What is Jesus's response?

7. What does Luke 10:27 teach us about loving God?

8. Jeremiah 31:3 describes God's love for you and me. What does it say?

9. God's love changes the way we respond to others. What does Ephesians 5:1–2 say?

10. Examine the words of 1 John 4:16.

7

Discovering Strength in Weakness

Celebrating Christ's Sufficiency

> I delight in weaknesses, in insults, in hardships, in persecutions, in difficulties. For when I am weak, then I am strong.
>
> 2 Corinthians 12:10

Can any of us truly "delight" in weakness, hardships, and such? If you think you have attained the attitude of the apostle Paul, try this simple test. Next time somebody insults you, just grin and declare, "Well, that was simply delightful!"

Feeling that way seems completely upside down to me. Yet Paul delighted not only in insults but in all kinds of problems and perplexing situations—the kind of cir-

cumstances that would send you and me into an all-out
tizzy. Look again at what delighted him: weaknesses, insults, hardships, persecutions, difficulties. Wow! That's
unbelievable!

At least it was to me until I looked up the actual meaning
of the words Paul used. See if these definitions help you
get a grasp on this hard-to-understand concept:

- Delight: not feeling giddy but choosing to think well
  of something, to see the good in it, and because you
  can see the "something good," to actually take pleasure in it.
- Weaknesses: being completely helpless in a given
  situation; feebleness of body or mind; frailty or
  limitations.
- Insults: bearing reproaches, injury, harm, or hurt; being
  the victim of insolence or disrespect.
- Hardships: dealing with the pressure of exter-
  nal circumstances; being unable to control what's
  happening.
- Persecutions: facing unjust criticism, harassment, or
  hostility; "being pursued."
- Difficulties: anguish, distress; being in a narrow place,
  a tight place, hemmed in, cramped, or confined.
- Strong: knowing that even though you don't feel
  strong and in spite of the difficulties you face, you
  are able, capable, and yes, even powerful enough to
  keep going.

How could Paul claim to "think well" of these kinds of
things? You may be thinking, *Well, duh, he was the apostle
Paul after all. His supersaint status gave him an extra measure
of grace.* Maybe you think he was insulated from the real

world, an ivory tower representative of early Christianity. Whatever you may be thinking, the truth is, Paul struggled with life just like you and I. In fact, he probably suffered more than any one of us ever has. Most of the time the great apostle quietly pressed on in spite of adversity, but occasionally he wrote about it, preserving in Scripture an account of his difficulties and more importantly providing inspiration and help for those of us who would follow in his steps.

One time, in defense of his status as an apostle, he reluctantly compared himself to others.

> I've worked much harder, been jailed more often, beaten up more times than I can count, and at death's door time after time. I've been flogged five times with the Jews' thirty-nine lashes, beaten by Roman rods three times, pummeled with rocks once. I've been shipwrecked three times, and immersed in the open sea for a night and a day. In hard traveling year in and year out, I've had to ford rivers, fend off robbers, struggle with friends, struggle with foes. I've been at risk in the city, at risk in the country, endangered by desert sun and sea storm, and betrayed by those I thought were my brothers. I've known drudgery and hard labor, many a long and lonely night without sleep, many a missed meal, blasted by the cold, naked to the weather.
>
> And that's not the half of it, when you throw in the daily pressures and anxieties of all the churches. When someone gets to the end of his rope, I feel the desperation in my bones. When someone is duped into sin, an angry fire burns in my gut.
>
> 2 Corinthians 11:23–29 Message

Can you identify with Paul? On even one point? Have you ever, for example, been insulted? I wish I could say no, but alas, I've experienced firsthand a few comments and found myself in more than a few situations that fall into that category.

One weekend I caught a plane in Dallas and headed to a women's conference. I was prepared, prayed up, and looking good—if I do say so myself—when I stepped off the plane and met the leadership team at the luggage carousel.

You know how it is when a bunch of excited women gang up to say hi to a long-awaited, eagerly anticipated guest. You may *not* know how it feels to be the guest, especially if you're the speaker—the one whose name is on the front of the advertisement brochures, whose picture is posted on the church walls. There's a special kind of angst that goes along with even limited "celebrity" status. Call it performance anxiety or just a touch of fear, the feeling prevails in my circle of writer-speaker friends. I know this for sure because we talk about it. The good thing is, once the introductions are done, the atmosphere changes. The conference becomes like a big family reunion as Christian sisterhood kicks in and funny stories abound.

On this particular afternoon, however, one sister said something that was NOT funny even though she may have been trying to be. She pushed through the circle, placed her hand on my arm, and spat out the *F* word. "I'm glad you are FAT because I know you'll be lots of fun." Even though I'll never forget what she said, I can't for the life of me remember what *I* said. I do, however, remember how I felt, and it definitely was not delight. But I'm glad to report that later, after a few quiet moments in my hotel room, God answered the question troubling me: *What in the world was* that *all about?*

I found myself wondering how many times I'd had preconceived notions about people, thinking in stereotypes instead of seeing them as they really are. Maybe I'd been indifferent to some who were less than classy and charming, those who didn't fit the upper-middle-class, well-educated-and-humorous pattern I so enjoy. Perhaps it had occurred more often than I'd been aware of or willing to admit, but it would *not* happen on this weekend! Throughout the conference, I felt a special sensitivity to those attending, along with a vivid awareness of the presence of God. I knew he was up to something good though I had no idea what it might be.[1] So I listened better than ever before, and I saw deeply into the souls of some women I might have at other times overlooked.

As incredible as it might seem, on Saturday afternoon as I rested on a chaise near the pool, the sister appeared, plopping into the chair next to me. I offered her one of my cookies. (Okay, her comments didn't hurt my appetite.) Then she began to talk. About her granddaughter's tattoos and piercings, about the teen's spiritual condition, about the baby (the woman's first great-grandbaby) the girl had given up for adoption just three weeks before. As she talked, occasionally dabbing her eyes with a tissue, I felt my heart soften. Then suddenly I began to "think well of" the insult she'd handed out earlier, for it had pushed open the door to real communication and created a place for God to come in and do his work in human hearts. As for the "pleasure" factor? Why, the wave of pure joy that washed over me just about swept me off my chair and into the pool! The Blessed Controller of All Circumstances had reminded me once again that when I am weak, wounded, and helpless, he is all-powerful.

---

*W*hen I am weak, then I am strong.

The Apostle Paul

As soul-stretching as that episode was to me, Paul apparently experienced something greater, for the word "insults" means more than some verbal assault. It includes "reproaches"—having someone distance themselves, shun, or slander you. I have a friend who knows from experience what that feels like.

For as long as Emily could remember, she'd been closer than a sister to her girlfriend Amy. (Again, I'm using pseudonyms here.) These two women shared the same interests in books, movies, and certain fun restaurants. But more importantly, they connected spiritually. Sharing biblical insights, opening up about their personal hurts, being able to talk about the things that brought them joy—these co-experiences bonded them deeply. I'm not saying the two friends never disagreed. The truth is, they had very different personalities and gifts. But whenever they didn't see eye to eye on an issue, they would playfully agree to disagree and move on, certain their friendship would stand the test of time.

One day Emily epitomized the depth of their bond when she laughed and said, "When we get old, let's move into the same nursing home. We'll need somebody to clip our toenails." But unfortunately, long before it was time to start shopping for a retirement community, life for these friends took a downward turn. Amy got caught in the snare of infidelity. At first it was only an emotional entanglement, but it developed rather quickly into an all-out affair. It's amazing to me how so many women get tangled in the same trap—the most effective weapon in Satan's arsenal, the only one he really needs to destroy a woman's family, her ministry, her self-respect.

For more than a year the friendship between Amy and Emily bobbled on troubled waters. Emily cried, prayed, and tried to help. Amy struggled painfully, her emotions flip-flopping between moments of ecstasy and days of guilt-laden despair. No matter how hard she tried to reconcile her feelings and, at times, to break free of the entanglement, her feet were caught in a ragged net pulling her down to the bottom of a murky sea. Eventually Amy grew tired of fighting the spiritual battle and made a determined choice, albeit a devastatingly wrong one. She got a divorce, left her family, and settled in a new community with a new husband. The friends suffered irreconcilable differences too. And lots of people were hurt in the process, including a large circle of extended family members, caring friends, and ministry partners.

During the following months, several attempts were made by both women to span the ever-widening gulf between them. But every time they tried to make things right, their different points of view stood like the proverbial elephant in the middle of the room. They couldn't move it, go around it, change it, or see over it. So once again they agreed to disagree. The only difference was, this time the discussion was not one bit playful. Eventually, it was Amy who chose to distance herself from Emily. "Don't call, don't write, don't even pray for me anymore. I no longer consider you my friend." To make matters worse, Emily began hearing of rumors, accusations, and judgment calls Amy was making about her to mutual friends and business associates.

I wonder if a similar "reproach" happened to Paul. Did one of his close friends or ministry partners distance himself? Was he the brunt of unjust criticism and gossip? Of course he was! You've just read his own account about some of it! Seems to me, Emily could identify with Paul on several points, including how it felt to see a friend surrender to the enemy: "When someone gets to the end of his rope, I feel the desperation in my bones. When someone is duped into sin, an angry fire burns in my gut" (2 Cor. 11:29 Message). Paul identified with those he loved, feeling their pain, suffering right alongside them, just as Emily had done with her friend.

Recently Emily said, "I'm still trying to process what happened, trying to figure out what, if anything, I need to do in the future." She gave a deep sigh and added, "I've never felt so helpless, so powerless as I did during that time." Is Emily "delighting" in the insults she received from her friend? Is she "taking pleasure" in them? Not really! Not yet! But she is coping well. Jesus fills the friendship void in Emily's life, and little by little her heart is being mended.

We can sometimes see more through a tear, than through a telescope.

Lord Byron

Most of us remember Paul writing about his thorn in the flesh. Apparently there was one thing, more than anything else, that he wanted to be relieved of. So he did what you and I do when we want relief. He asked God. In fact he asked again and again and again. Three times he came before the Father, begging him to take the "whatever" away. Do you remember God's answer? In short, it was no. But not because our benevolent God wanted to see his beloved servant suffer needlessly. Not because he didn't care. But because he was doing something bigger and greater— something in Paul's heart that could not be accomplished in a thornless environment. Paul didn't understand at the time. I'm not sure I do even now, at least not completely.

But I'm thinking it was so people like you and me could learn how life really works.

Remember the story of Paul's last voyage to Rome (see Acts 27)? With all its tragedy and triumph, it reveals the drama of human life. It's everybody's story. Most of us set sail with optimism and hope, desiring to reach a safe harbor. But like Paul's trip, ours involves a strange mixture of pain and problems along with God's provision and protection. We're tossed about on troubled seas, we face all kinds of opposition among our "crew," and we sometimes find ourselves washed up on some sandbar that completely stops our forward progress. Sometimes we experience a major shipwreck. When that happens, we suddenly become better listeners, smarter "sailors," and, in general, more compliant people. And no matter how dark and cold the waters that threaten us, God always provides an anchor, a lifeboat, or a piece of our own broken vessel, as a "way of escape" so we can make it safely to shore.[2]

> There are no gains without pains.
>
> J.C. Ryle

The Upside-Down Truth...

Thorns help us more than they hurt us. But none of us like them! If I had my way, I'd have roses with nary a prickly spot on their long stems. I'd have a soft world, a happy place in which to live, a sky without clouds, mountaintops without valleys, etc., etc., etc. I think what I'm really longing for is heaven. Problem is, I want it right now. I want the sheer joy of heaven without having to endure even one pain in preparation for it. Now, before you criticize my lack of patience, isn't that what you really want too?

Nevertheless, I have enough spiritual savvy, and you do too, to know that if we had it our way, heaven would be a different kind of place than God designed it to be. For one thing, there'd be no need for victory songs and happy dances, no need to celebrate having overcome. And that would mean less joy, less praise, less adoration for the one who conquered our enemy, took away sin, and brought us safely home.

---

*T*he pain now is part of the happiness then.
C. S. Lewis

So as we learn to walk through the thorny places here on earth, we will probably deal with it like Paul did—accepting by faith that there's a reason for every problem, learning to be thankful "in everything" (1 Thess. 5:18 NKJV) and "for everything" (Eph. 5:20), and finding God's grace sufficient. Read Paul's testimony:

> So I wouldn't get a big head, I was given the gift of a handicap to keep me in constant touch with my limitations. Satan's angel did his best to get me down; what he in fact did was push me to my knees. No danger then of walking around high and mighty! At first I didn't think of it as a gift, and begged God to remove it. Three times I did that, and then he told me,
>
> > My grace is enough; it's all you need.
> > My strength comes into its own in your weakness.
>
> Once I heard that, I was glad to let it happen. I quit focusing on the handicap and began appreciating the gift. It was a case of Christ's strength moving in on my weakness. Now I take limitations in stride, and with good cheer, these

limitations that cut me down to size—abuse, accidents, opposition, bad breaks. I just let Christ take over! And so the weaker I get, the stronger I become.

2 Corinthians 12:7–10 Message

Did you get what he said? His problems were *a gift* to him—"so I wouldn't get a big head . . . to keep me in constant touch with my limitations . . . to push me to my knees." No wonder Paul could find pleasure in his thorn, for it had brought him to a place of complete trust. Isn't that what happens with most of us? We feel strong until problems come. When they multiply or come at us from all sides, we finally realize that we must have the strong current of Jesus's supernatural strength flowing through us in order to survive. When we grasp the truth of his presence and power, we really can be grateful, just as Paul was, "so that Christ's power may rest on [us]" (2 Cor. 12:9). Perhaps that's why he could live by a truth that seems upside down to most of us.

If I must boast, I will boast of the things that show my weakness.

2 Corinthians 11:30 Message

I can't imagine my friend Christie boasting about anything, but she's not ashamed to admit her weaknesses. Recently she said, "Everything happens for a purpose. I don't think we are supposed to keep our story to ourselves, especially when it might help somebody else." So indulge me, if you would, while I brag on her.

Christie grew up in a home where she was often neglected and forced to assume adult responsibilities when she was just a little girl. She had little connection with her peers. Every day after school she would rush home to clean the house and prepare supper before her mom and dad got home from work. "When I'd get home," Christy confided, "there would be a package of meat thawing on the counter. It was up to me to decide what to do with it."

It was the ground meat that posed the biggest problem for the youngster. Usually she settled on some sort of hash or Hamburger Helper. She always had the table set, the water glasses full, and the meal waiting on the stove right on time. Huge responsibility for a child, huh?

To make her childhood even more miserable, Christie had a nagging health problem. At the risk of sounding indelicate (and I share this with Christie's permission), she had worms. Yep, those little white parasites kids get from playing in the sandbox or from eating with unwashed hands. It's not a serious medical condition, but it is a pesky, yucky one—one requiring a doctor's visit and a round of medicine. It's tragic to think that Christie was too scared to tell her distant and austere mother, and so she lived with worms for five years. But the worst part was that, throughout all those years, Christie thought she was dying. In the mind of a child, what else could such a thing mean?

By the time she'd reached sixteen, Christie had put back enough money from her meager allowance to pay for a gutsy move. She called a doctor and made an appointment. Sitting in his office, she swallowed her tears and told him what was going on. "Why, that's no problem," he responded compassionately. "I'll write a prescription to take care of it."

No problem? What?

Talk about getting a new lease on life! Christie was beside herself. She got the prescription filled and, lo and behold,

within a few days all was well. At least everything was okay physically. Becoming
emotionally and spiritually well would
take many more years.

The inevitable questions we ask
when hearing about such childhood abuse are, where were the extended family members? Were her
teachers, neighbors, and friends
clueless? And, the most nagging
question of all, where was God?
Where was our loving, compassionate, heavenly Father when one
of his little children was enduring
such misery?

The Upside-Down Truth...

The weaker
I get,
the
stronger
I become.

The Apostle Paul

To queries like these I throw up my
hands and declare, I do not know! Seems
to me, that's where faith comes in. When I
don't understand, then I choose to trust, hanging
on to the things I know for sure. And this I know. In all
her weakness, frailty, injury, hardships, and distress—in
all her tight places—Christie grew spiritually and became
strong.

Her inner strength became obvious to everybody who
knew her when an unspeakable tragedy happened in her
family. In a fit of despair, her brother took his own life. Christie was devastated when she called with the awful news. I
cried with her and prayed silently that the trauma would
not weaken her faith. I knew my prayers were answered
when I saw her at the funeral a couple of days later. With
dignity and grace, Christie served the other members of the
grief-stricken family, including her mother and daddy, and
her brother's twelve-year-old son, who couldn't bear the

thought that his daddy was gone. I stood outside the tent and prayed as she escorted her parents to their chairs and whispered words of comfort to the disconsolate child.

That evening my thoughts went back to the first time I'd met Christie. Still plagued by timidity and insecurity, she had simply needed an older woman to talk to. Her best friend, Sandy, introduced us. Christie showed me pictures of her husband and three-year-old daughter and talked freely about the complicated issues she'd faced growing up. Her face brightened when she revealed that she'd become a Christian. Eager to grow, she had settled into a small Baptist church.

"Gracie," she confided, "one day I was sitting in a circle in my Sunday school class, not wanting to draw attention to myself, but feeling like I was wearing a clown suit and big red shoes with tassels on the toes. Somebody prayed, then the teacher said a person's name—actually the name 'John.' Then she muttered a few numbers—'one, twelve.' Everybody started flipping through the Bible, and I had no idea what they were doing."

At this point I couldn't keep from interrupting, "Oh, Christie, what did you do?"

"I ducked my head and started thumbing through the pages. I'd never felt so lost. But when I got home, I looked through my Bible and discovered it was written in books with chapters and verses numbered in sequence." Christie tucked a strand of her long brown hair behind her ear as a broad smile spread across her face.

As you can imagine, my heart went out to this beautiful girl with such limited knowledge of the things I knew so well. After that, we got together regularly. I bought a bookmark at the Christian bookstore that listed all sixty-six books of the Bible. I helped her memorize them. She taught me how to remove crayon markings off wallpaper.

We had long conversations while sipping tall glasses of iced tea at her kitchen table. Christie and I really loved each other—and we liked each other too.

Eventually, as one phase of life morphed into another, we both moved away from the small Texas town where we had met, and for more than a dozen years we completely lost contact. Then one evening at a birthday party for our mutual friend Sandy, we spotted each other and ran into a big bear hug. And our conversation picked up right where it left off more than a decade before. Isn't that the way it is with true friendship? The bond doesn't come unglued just because you're apart for a while. As dinner was served and the buzz of conversation picked up, Christie added generous helpings of laughter and funny stories to the nourishing mix. My young friend had not only grown spiritually, she'd developed a great sense of humor. After that, I couldn't wait to see her again. Before long, I would have a chance to do just that.

A few weeks after our reunion, Christie heard through that same mutual friend that I was going through a difficult and hurtful family matter. She called, suggesting the three of us meet for a day of shopping, lunch, and chocolate, thus providing the perfect solution to my problems.

As we strolled through the Grapevine Mills Mall, Christie and Sandy listened as I unloaded a tangled mess of feelings. Soon afterward, while we shared lunch at Steak n Shake, I realized I'd just experienced a great role reversal. I was no longer a mentor-mom to Christie. She was counseling me! We were sisters—sisters in Christ walking hand in hand.

When we finished our burgers, we shared a double chocolate fudge brownie topped with vanilla ice cream and hot fudge. By the time we rested our three spoons in the empty bowl, I was feeling really good!

*C*hocolate isn't the answer to all life's problems, just the ones concerning men, money, work, parents, friends, travel, shopping, taxes . . .

Barbara Johnson

It could have been the overload of caffeine killed off a few of my brain cells, because the events that followed revealed a definite mental deficit on my part. When the waitress delivered the bill, I grabbed the ticket, located my credit card, and quipped, "My hubby can pay for this." (It's a line that always gets a good laugh and usually settles the argument about who will pay.)

But when I handed it to the waitress, she said I had to pay at the front register. I tucked the bill and credit card in the fold of my wallet and laid it on the table. Then we continued to talk and talk and talk. When they started mopping the floors around our feet, we decided to leave. I scooped up the wallet and stuffed it into my purse, and we headed toward my car, jabbering all the way.

Later that evening at Dillard's, I opened my wallet and discovered that I had NOT paid for our food! Of course I would go back and make things right. But, easily distracted woman that I am, it took a couple of days to get around to it.

When I finally pushed through the door and located our waitress, she hollered, "I knew you'd come back. You gals were too nice not to come back. Nobody else thought you would!" Well, it may have taken awhile for right to prevail, but when it did, God poured out his blessing. I felt good knowing I'd done the right thing, the waitress's faith was rewarded, and she got a ten-dollar tip—my guilt offering!

I couldn't wait to tell Christie and Sandy what had happened. A few days later I received a funny handmade card in the mail. Christie had drawn caricatures of the three of us bolting toward our car, with me waving my wallet in the air and bellowing, "Let's get out of here. My hubby can pay for our food!"

Christie's life, just like Paul's, like Amy's and Emily's, as well as yours and mine, is a mixture of perplexing problems and God's provision. Overwhelming difficulties and amazing solutions. Mind-boggling confusion and laugh-till-you-snort fun. Personal weakness and divine strength.

Mrs. Charles Cowman, in her classic work *Streams in the Desert*, wrote a literal translation of the verse this chapter is based upon. It gives an amazing new emphasis and unusual power to the familiar words: "Therefore I take pleasure in being without strength, in insults, in being pinched, in being chased about, in being cooped up in a corner for Christ's sake; for when I am without strength, then am I *dynamite*."[3]

It's comforting to know that as we move from one phase of life to another, in all our weaknesses, Jesus is with us, filling us with his supercharged, always effective, absolutely explosive power. And isn't it exciting to think of ourselves as dynamite?

$\mathcal{R}$ight-Side Up

1. Romans 12:12 offers us three ways to stay centered even when difficulties multiply. What are those three concepts?

2. In 1 Corinthians 1:27–29, whom did God choose? Why did he choose them?

3. Compare 1 Corinthians 1:31 to 2 Corinthians 11:30. Do these claims mean the same thing? Why or why not?

4. Read Jeremiah 9:23–24. What did Jeremiah write about boasting? How do these words compare with what Paul wrote in 2 Corinthians 11:30?

5. What does God promise in 2 Corinthians 9:8? Note the repeated use of the word "all." Why do you think the Holy Spirit inspired Paul to write this word again and again?

6. What is the promise of Isaiah 43:2? Write the verse, one phrase at a time, or try to diagram the sentence in the following space. Memorize the verse and meditate on it.

7. In this chapter you read the story of Paul's thorn in the flesh. You may have thought it was his only problem, the only thing keeping him from living a trouble-free existence. But in 2 Corinthians 12:10 he lists five additional "thorns." What were they? Do you have some of the same problems? Which one troubles you most? Decide how you can handle it better.

8

Finding Joy in Trials

Coming to Terms
with Suffering Loss, Feeling Pain

Consider it pure joy, my brothers, whenever you face trials
of many kinds.

James 1:2

I think I've come to terms with the fact that all of us will, at
one time or another, face trials. What seems upside down
to me is "considering it pure joy." But that is what James
is saying here. And as difficult as that might be, it is a lot
easier to do than what Peter suggests when he instructs us
to "greatly rejoice" (which literally means "jump up and
down for joy") smack in the middle of our distress (1 Peter
1:6 NASB).

Thankfully Peter goes on to explain that trials come to prove our faith. Just like gold is refined by fire and emerges a stronger, purer, more radiant substance, our lives will be tested and, in the end, will produce a blessed result: "praise and glory and honor at the revelation of Jesus Christ" (1 Peter 1:7 NASB). When we think of our trials that way, we really can consider them something "precious." And thinking forward to the time when Jesus will be fully revealed brings to most of us a burst of great joy.

The trials mentioned by both James and Peter include things that happen to us completely outside our control as well as temptations that come from inside ourselves. Either way, whether they come from the outside in or the inside out, all of them create a certain amount of pressure; and pressure, as uncomfortable as it may seem at the time, is good for us.

Long before the days of microwave ovens and fast-food restaurants, there was the pressure cooker. My mother had one. It was a quick way to cook Sunday dinner before it was time to head off to church. In a weekly ritual, my mom would brown a big roast in the heavy-duty cooker, then pour in a small amount of water. I can still remember the sizzle as that water bounced around the sides of the pan, sending up a blast of steam. Before all the steam could escape, she would grab the lid and lock it on tight. Then she'd slip a pressure gauge over the vent on top and watch as the needle moved upward. When just the right amount of pressure had built up inside, she'd adjust the flame on the stove and in less than an hour the roast would be done.

The pressure cooker was a real boon to yesterday's homemaker, but it did have a downside. One misstep in the process, like not getting the top locked down or allowing too much steam to build up, and Sunday dinner could end up on the ceiling. Worse yet, my mother told me scary stories of people getting burned by all that steam. Usually when Mom started cooking, I'd run in the next room until the roast was locked up so tight it couldn't get away.

So why would a person use a gadget like a pressure cooker, considering the risks involved? For one thing it was quick. Even in those much less complicated days, women looked for shortcuts and time-savers. Besides that, the food that pressure cooker turned out was beyond excellent. All the flavor and natural juices were literally locked into the meat, and it was tender—the most tender roast beef you've ever stuck a fork into.

Is that what our heavenly Father is trying to accomplish in our lives? Is it important to him that our heart become tenderized? The author of Ephesians thought so: "Be kind to one another, tender-hearted, forgiving each other, just as God in Christ also has forgiven you" (Eph. 4:32 NASB). I wonder if that kind of tenderness is even possible without a person doing a certain amount of simmering in life's pressure cooker.

What kind of pressure are you facing right now? Is the pain intense, the fire really hot? If so, you can be sure the process is tenderizing you, making you into a softer, kinder, gentler woman. There's not a single one of us who would want to jump into a pot of hot water or flippantly say turn up the fire, but when we realize the good result, we can honestly find joy in our pain. Isn't that what James meant when he wrote "consider it all joy"? He is not asking us to be thrilled or even to feel good; instead, he invites us to honestly think it through and be thankful.

Things were not perfect for the apostle Paul when he wrote Philippians. In fact, he was in a dark, cold prison. But in spite of the hurtful conditions, he didn't write doom and gloom. The words he penned are full of joy: "Rejoice in the Lord always. I will say it again: Rejoice!" (Phil. 4:4). Paul had discovered something women like you and I need to know. We do not have to be a prisoner of our circumstances, no matter how difficult or confining they may be. We can rise above them by learning to rejoice in the Lord.

The most beautiful stones have been tossed by the wind and washed by the water and polished to brilliance over time.

Anonymous

Pressure not only tenderizes our hearts but proves whether or not we are genuine. Have you ever been through a difficult time of testing and made it? Maybe you even passed the test with an A. If you have, you know something about finding joy in trials. What a soul-satisfying thing to know that we can endure, to know that when future tests and temptations come, we have what it takes to overcome. Trials help us understand ourselves better, including the most important discovery of all—knowing whether or not our faith is the real thing. "Examine yourselves to see whether or not you are in the faith; test yourselves. Do you not realize that Christ Jesus is in you—unless, of course, you fail the test?" (2 Cor. 13:5).

My friend Pat has a diamond ring that's so big and brilliant it almost blinds you when the sunlight catches it just right. Now, I'm not the least bit envious. I'm not much of a bling-bling person myself, but I do appreciate fine things on other women. Especially when it's someone as nice and unassuming as Pat.

A few years ago, Pat and I and several other girlfriends went to Seattle and spent almost a week together in a condominium in the Cascade Mountains. We shopped at Pikes Place Market, drank huge amounts of Seattle's Best Coffee, and ate at the classiest restaurants we could find. And Pat wore her ring. I couldn't help but notice it because, well, Pat uses hand signals when she talks and punctuates every sentence with a wave of her fork. To be honest, there were times that diamond just about put my eye out. One day I mentioned it. "Pat, that ring is simply beautiful, the way it picks up the light—"

"Oh, Gracie," she interrupted, "this is not my real ring. It's a CZ. I don't take *real* diamonds on a trip like this."

Well, I do declare! The ring was a fake. But to my untrained eye it looked real. It sparkled real. And besides that, it was designed like the original—similar setting, same size stone. . . . Hmmm, I'd been duped!

I couldn't quit thinking about that ring and how easily I'd been fooled. So when we got back home, I booted up my computer and did a little research. Apparently it takes an expert with a high-powered monocle and a well-trained eye to tell the difference between a good-quality cubic zirconia and a real diamond. Why, if I had those two rings, chances are I'd never get it right. I'd end up wearing the diamond to the fish market and the fake to a party! But you know what? Even though a phony diamond can easily fool someone like me who's depending on a simple "sight" test, a CZ wouldn't fool anybody if it were put to the "pressure" test. No matter how good the fake might be, it just wouldn't stand up to the stress.

Pat's CZ would be crushed under pressure, but Pat herself has been thoroughly tested and passed with flying colors. Her son, Mark, was only seventeen when he was murdered

at the hands of a drugged-out schoolmate. Grief
almost overwhelmed my friend. She spent
many an afternoon strolling through the
cemetery and picking at the flowers
that marked her son's grave. It was
a safe place to cry and talk to God.
And talk she did. Unashamed to
reveal her feelings to her heavenly Father, she freely asked every
question that came to her mind, including *why*. Why did God allow
such a thing to happen?

*Happiness
comes when
good things
happen;
joy remains
no matter
what
happens.*

The Upside-Down Truth...

When Pat told me about Mark's
death more than fifteen years after
it happened, she admitted something
more. "Gracie, I even talked to Mark
during those trips to his grave. It was very
therapeutic, airing out my hurt, and expressing my feelings. I told him how much I missed
him and loved him. I wasn't trying to connect in a mystical
way, but somehow it made me feel close to him and eased
the awful pain I felt." As I listened, Pat smiled and added,
"Now don't think I'm crazy, but on Mother's Day less than
two months after he died, I heard Mark's voice. It wasn't
out loud but in my heart. *Mom, stop grieving over my body. I
never liked my body much anyway.* I stopped crying and stood
very still. *Mom, you wouldn't believe the colors that are here,
and the flowers that are here. It's just beautiful.*"

When Pat finished her sentence, I sat silent, awestruck.
No wonder she'd kept the story to herself so many years.
Some things are just too precious, too intimate, too holy to
be shared lightly. Finally Pat spoke again. "Gracie, I know
psychologists would say it was psychosomatic—that I

heard what I wanted to hear. But I believe that sometimes God gives a glimpse into heaven."

Pat's attitude changed after that. Not that she didn't grieve. Not that she didn't continue to miss her only son. But peace prevailed in her heart because she knew Mark was in a better, perfectly beautiful place. She felt a measure of genuine joy in knowing he wouldn't want to come back to planet Earth even if he could. A smile crossed Pat's face when she thought about Mark's new body that had no weaknesses or limitations. She imagined him strolling down streets of gold with his hands in his pockets.

Since that time Pat has studied, researched, and compiled a notebook full of insights on heaven. Occasionally she teaches a class on the subject. It's a course that helps earth-travelers like you and me look away from the problems and perplexities of life to a land of eternal blessing. And that brings joy to student and teacher alike. When we choose to focus on eternity, it changes everything we experience today, including our broken hearts.

An eternal perspective
is the only perspective God has.
Unknown

Pat is not the only Christian who's been encouraged by a peek into eternity. T. W. Hunt, in *From Heaven's View*, writes of an unusual experience he had after his wife's death, sort of like Paul's third heaven experience.[1] Dr. Hunt discusses the changes in our sensory perception. "The most unusual aspect of the experience consisted of the colors—colors that did not exist on earth. I saw flowers in colors far more dazzling than any crimson I had ever seen in the world. In spite of the wide range of colors, they blended into works of art unlike any I have ever seen in the Louvre. In some strange way my entire body participated in the sublime details of those masterworks. My senses cooperated to engulf me in sheer pleasure."[2]

Dr. Hunt explains why heaven's colors will be more vivid than any we've known earth-side:

> Our senses, including our sense of light, will be far more acute than they are on this earth. Why? Our eyes see a re-markably tiny portion of the enormous spectrum of light that instruments can register. Color results from the length of the light wave which can be extremely long or almost immeasurably short. Of all the waves, the longest we can perceive is red, then orange, yellow, green, blue, violet, and then . . . , our faculties stop functioning. But there are still colors in infrared waves which are invisible to our eyes. After that comes microwaves and then the longest of all— radio waves, but our eyes are not designed to see them.
>
> Our range of hearing is limited also. We are able to per-ceive sound waves in a narrow spectrum. Elephants and whales can hear long waves, below our capacity to hear; dogs and bats can hear short waves, above our capacity to hear. When we arrive in heaven we will be aware of new and intensely pleasurable colors, sounds, and smells in our new environment. Our senses will have been changed to allow us to fully enjoy the beauty and delights of heaven.[3]

Perhaps the only glimpse you and I will ever get into heaven (on this side, at least) is by reading the aging apostle John's vision. At one point he saw God seated on his throne. An aura of infinite beauty and matchless colors surrounded him. John seemed to have trouble putting it into words. And no wonder. Most of us think of God being clothed in pure, glistening, white light. But John described a colorful

God. "Immediately I was in the Spirit; and behold, a throne was standing in heaven, and One sitting on the throne. And He who was sitting was like a jasper stone and a sardius in appearance; and there was a rainbow around the throne, like an emerald in appearance" (Rev. 4:2–3 NASB).

Later he described a city where the streets are gold and the walls are jasper two hundred feet thick.[4] The walls rest on foundation stones adorned with precious jewels including jasper, sapphire, chalcedony, emerald, sardonyx, sardius, chrysolite, beryl, topaz, chrysoprase, jacinth, and amethyst.[5] Some of these stones are recognizable to us. But some of them are not. Seems we'll have to wait for our eyes to be opened before we can even know what they are, much less enjoy their brilliant color.

So, does all this talk of heaven really make things better while we live in today's world? Of course it does. Jesus was able to endure the cross, putting aside the shame he naturally felt, because of the joy he knew was coming—the joy of being in heaven with his Father, the joy of sharing heaven's trouble-free environment with those of us who would join him later.[6] Near the time of his death and departure, Jesus encouraged his confused, frightened disciples by helping them focus on heaven. He pulled them aside and said, "There is plenty of room for you in my Father's home. . . . I'm on my way to get your room ready, I'll come back and get you so you can live where I live" (John 14:2–3 Message). On another occasion, he said, "In the world you will have tribulation;

The Upside-Down Truth...

If you live for present comfort, trials will make you bitter. If you live for future glory, trials will make you better.

but be of good cheer, I have overcome the world" (John 16:33 NKJV).

Someday we too will celebrate having overcome the world and will spend eternity basking in our glorious new surroundings, enjoying unbroken fellowship with Jesus. Just the thought of it is enough to make a gal like me with a bad knee want to jump up and down with joy. In the meantime, as we live day by day, we can sample a foretaste of glory—right here, right now.

This is the day the LORD has made;
let us rejoice and be glad in it.

Psalm 118:24

Recently I met a friend for coffee (yep, at Starbucks). As we sipped our grande latte and sampled a pumpkin cupcake, Gayle talked about her feelings. A writer with a vivid imagination, Gayle really knows how to express herself. With her children grown, my friend has reached a change-point in her life with more time to pursue her own interests, follow her own heart. "Gracie," she began, "now that I'm moving into midlife, I find myself wanting more. You know, more of God, more adventure, more excitement, more music, more beauty, more sex, more color." Gayle grinned and her cheeks took on a bit of a glow. (After all, she'd just blurted out the *S* word!) "I even want more challenges, more risk."

I smiled as I thought, *Me too!*

Does Gayle speak for you?

Do you, for example, want more color in your life? I do. I want splashes of coral, magenta, azure blue, and a touch of fuchsia. The thought of living a life chock-full of bright, vibrant, living color brings me joy, even if some of the colors test my spiritual strength.

Even our trials don't come to us dressed in gray tones. When James warned us to expect "trials of many kinds," he was actually saying they would present themselves to us in brilliant, mind-popping color. It makes sense when we realize that the legitimate desires of our heart, our dreams, our drive to excel, and even our longings to reach certain spiritual heights are the very areas where we'll be tested, maybe tempted to sin.

The word James used (translated "various" in the NASB) also means "varied" or "variegated." It suggests having many colors, like the multicolored blouse I tried on at the Liz Claiborne outlet. (I absolutely loved the bright stripes.) Peter selected the very same word when he wrote about temptations, and Moses used it when he described Joseph's coat of many colors in the book of Genesis.[7]

We writers get really picky about words, going to great lengths to select just the right one. If you don't believe me, just sit down at the local coffee shop and listen to a couple of writers buzz about words! Anyway, James, succinct writer that he was, picked exactly the right one.

So, what's your point? you may be thinking. *What difference does it make?*

For one thing, I'm wondering why so many Christians think in black and white when throughout the centuries of time God has inspired men like Moses and James and Peter to write about life in Technicolor. Who says life is black and white with shades of gray between? The truth is, life is painted from a palette of vibrant colors including various colors of trials, tests, and temptations. We use colors to express these things all the time. We say that a person is green with jealousy and envy. Sometimes, when we're sick, we claim to be green—around the gills. If we're feeling good, we are "in the pink." When depressed we say a person's feeling blue. We all know that "red in the face" means anger. And yellow describes a person who's less-than-courageous or downright cowardly. Shades of gray? That just doesn't say it for me!

Another reason I'm belaboring the point is to illustrate something amazing about God's grace. It comes in multiple colors too. It was Peter who revealed this to us when he used that word "various" again. He challenges women like you and me to deal with the complexities of life by "faithfully administering God's grace in its various forms" (1 Peter 4:10). In all its bright, colorful forms!

The verse also teaches us a creative, proactive way to help other women as we help ourselves. Our lives will be full of joy, even as multicolored trials swirl around us, if we'll focus on serving others, using our gifts, sharing our dreams with those who are living gray, vanilla-flavored lives. No matter what color the problems might be—whether they're red-hot, melancholy blue, or pea green—there's a matching shade of grace. Grace that provides a way of escape when we're tempted to sin, grace that covers like a warm blanket when we stumble and fall, grace that comforts and sustains us.

We do not have to be a victim of what's happening around us. Sometimes it is right to change our circumstances, to get out of a tight spot, or to bring in a trusted friend or counselor to ease the pressure. If we can't change things, we can make life easier by filling it with touches of glory and grace. That may take various forms:

- Find a way to make new friends. Try a new group at church. Join a book club at the library. Take time to visit a neighbor.

- Take a trip (it doesn't have to be far away and fancy—try a personal retreat at a nearby B&B).
- Treat yourself to lunch at your favorite restaurant. If you can't find a girlfriend to join you, go alone, take a book, linger over coffee and dessert, preferably something chocolate. (Now, don't minimize this suggestion. Believe me, there are times it feels fabulous to have a person wait on you, refill your water glass, speak kindly to you—even if you have to pay them to do it.)
- Spend some time outside. Take a walk in the sunshine, sit in the park, enjoy a sidewalk coffee shop.
- Most importantly, guard your heart. Get alone with God. Pray. Meditate on God's promises, soak in his truth.

Someday in heaven surrounded by more light and radiant color than we can imagine, we'll celebrate the fact that God's grace really has been sufficient. Imagine bowing before him, basking in the bright celestial light radiating from God's throne. Brilliant colors bouncing off the city walls and bejeweled foundation stones will cast a glow around the throne like a rainbow. And at that moment we will know that we are here because of God's multicolored grace.

Maybe that's the very reason this colorful heaven will feel so much like home.

Right-Side Up

1. Romans 5:1–5 gives several reasons why Christians are able to rejoice, even when things seem to be going wrong. List some of the reasons joy is possible.

2. List the qualities that are produced in our lives through these trials. Discuss these in your group or meditate upon them privately. Look up the meaning of the words.

3. What advice does Peter give in 1 Peter 4:12–13? How does he describe trials? Do you think this is a good description?

4. In Matthew 5:11–12, under what difficult circumstances did Jesus tell his disciples to rejoice? Why is this possible?

5. Having an "attitude of gratitude" makes all the difference in how we view life and how we handle adversity. Read Psalm 136. Which verses mean the most to you? How does this change your focus?

6. In 1 Corinthians 2:9 Paul writes about heaven's impact on our senses. What does he say?

9

Seeing Light
in the Darkness

How Faith Sheds Light
on Real-Life, Tough Issues

> We live by faith, not by sight.
>
> 2 Corinthians 5:7

Most of us are skeptical.

We trust what we can see or touch or feel.

We believe in people we know and feel most comfortable in situations we can handle. We love staying in our routine, eating the comfort food we grew up on, cuddling under our own warm blankets, and living in houses that are built on firm foundations. We want all our relationships to be cozy, so we cluster in groups of friends who think like we do.

If something messes up our plans, if friendship falters or our health fails, we want to fix it and fix it quick. When disaster happens, we try to solve the problem, change the circumstances, or remove the obstacles, so that life can proceed as usual. When something unexplainable happens—some bizarre accident, the death of a loved one, an unexpected divorce, the loss of a job or our reputation—we talk about finding closure, thinking we'll feel better if things are resolved, closed, finished.

Reason says, "Seeing is believing." Faith says, "Believing is seeing."

But what if we can't find closure? What if, no matter how hard we try, we see no earthly good in a thing? No greater purpose? What if we see nothing of eternal value in what has happened?

Isn't that where faith comes in? When we cannot see? Is that why Paul reminded us that "we live by faith, not by sight"? Because as difficult as it may seem, as upside down as it feels, sometimes faith is the only solid ground, the only substantive thing we have. "Faith is the substance of things hoped for, the evidence of things not seen" (Heb. 11:1 NKJV).

As I am writing this I can't help but think of the natural disasters that have occurred recently. Tsunamis, earthquakes, hurricanes, and floods. How do we handle things that are completely out of our control? Things that knock our feet out from under us? What happens if the Rock of Gibraltar crumbles? What happens when there's no solid ground to stand upon?

It is then, and sometimes only then, that we really live by faith. We grab hold of the spiritual realities we've based our

The Upside-Down Truth...

life upon when things were going well. We seek God. "The fundamental fact of existence is that this trust in God, this faith, is the firm foundation under everything that makes life worth living. It's our handle on what we can't see" (Heb. 11:1 Message).

I have two sons who live in the Houston area. When Hurricane Rita was bearing down on the Texas coast, meteorologists predicted the path of the storm. It would come ashore near Galveston, whip through Houston's Galleria area, and travel up Interstate 45, sweeping through The Woodlands on its trek northward. If the prognosticators were right, both Jason and Mike along with our daughter-in-law, Jeanna, and grandsons, Montana and Myles, were in jeopardy. They stockpiled water and filled the tanks of both cars with gasoline. Jason decided to head inland and wait out the storm with his older brother.

He called as he was loading his personal possessions into the back of his car. It's interesting what he gathered up—the photo album I'd compiled when he graduated from high school, his journals (yes, he inherited the writer's gene from his mother), his laptop, his new cell phone, a few favorite clothes, a blanket, and some bottles of water. It's also interesting what he did *not* put in the car. No mention of his stereo equipment, his color TV, not even his rather large and much-loved CD collection. He wrapped them in plastic and left them in his living room. Then, after he moved his motorcycle to higher ground, he started driving, joining almost two million other drivers who were evacuating the coast.

It took Jason six hours to make the forty-five-mile journey from downtown Houston to The Woodlands. When he arrived, Mike and Jeanna were making a critical decision. The sky was dark, the clouds ominous as wind whipped

the huge trees in their yard. Jeanna's mother had been calling from Idaho, and her brother, who lives east of Dallas,
was upset by the news he'd seen on TV. New Orleans's
Hurricane Katrina, with its horrible devastation and high
floodwaters, was on everybody's mind. So they all put
their heads together and came up with a plan. Her brother
and his friend who owns a private plane would pick up
Jeanna and the kids and fly them to a safer place. Mike and
Jason battened down the house, nailing plywood over the
south-side windows. Then they ushered the pets inside
and waited for the storm to hit.

As I watched the drama unfold on my television, I'd
never felt so helpless. There was not one thing I could do
to help my kids. Most of the time I couldn't even talk to
them as communications jammed and power lines were
downed. I prayed and waited to hear some news.

Do you know what happened next? The hurricane
changed directions. Instead of hitting the Houston area,
it came ashore near Port Arthur and Lake Charles, then
swept inland through Beaumont, wreaking havoc with its
two-hundred-mile-per-hour winds.

We mortals are powerless when it comes to the weather.
We can't control it; we can't understand it. Even with all
our equipment and expertise, we can't predict it.

Nevertheless, I was relieved for the sake of my loved ones
(albeit a bit perturbed at all our needless preparations and
angst). But I'd no sooner taken a deep breath when I heard
that my best friend's daughter who lived in Beaumont lost
her house and most of her possessions. One family safe and
sound. Another grieving an awful loss. Talk about mixed
emotions. I didn't know what to feel!

So what's a mother to do in a situation like this? What's
anybody to do when there's no way to make sense of things

that happen? Throw up our hands and give up? Or simply let God be God. Trust God without terms. Perhaps the author of Hebrews says it best when he writes simply, "By faith we understand . . ." (Heb. 11:3).

What we can never figure out by human reasoning, we are able to comprehend because of our faith. Following that declaration the writer goes on to list many different crises and perplexing situations that come to good people in what's been called Faith's Hall of Fame.[1] Almost every verse begins with the words "by faith." He lists problems and circumstances that nobody can accept apart from faith—God's people facing death and persecution, disasters, mind-boggling circumstances, and hard-to-understand issues of life. The truth is, there's much in life that doesn't make sense without faith. Today, we live our lives as the aforementioned heroes did: they "saw him who is invisible" (Heb. 11:27).

Just knowing that God is good, that he does all things well, is the light we need to illuminate the darkest corners of our world. When the earth shifts beneath our feet, we can hold on to the truth that encouraged the psalmist. "Therefore we will not fear, though the earth should change and though the mountains slip into the heart of the sea" (Ps. 46:2 NASB). He could say this because his confidence was in God alone, not even in something as stable and sure as planet Earth. "God is our refuge and strength, a very present help in trouble" (Ps. 46:1 NASB).

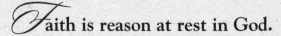

*F*aith is reason at rest in God.
Charles Spurgeon

We can learn a lot about faith by taking a look at the life of Habakkuk, one of the prophets of Israel. This little-known person with a funny name faced the same kind of problems we face today. And in the midst of them, he had his share of doubts, fears, questions, a few victories, and a growing faith.

He wrote about the society in which he lived, expressing his feelings to God. "Must I forever see this sin and misery all around me? Wherever I look, I see destruction and violence. I am surrounded by people who love to argue and fight. The law has become paralyzed and useless, and there is no justice given in the courts. The wicked far outnumber the righteous, and justice is perverted with bribes and trickery" (Hab. 1:3–4 NLT). Don't miss the long laundry list of problems: violence, sin, misery, lawlessness, perverted justice, bribes, trickery, and, if those adjectives weren't enough, he adds the term *wickedness*: "the wicked far outnumber the righteous." What a sorry state Israel was in!

Does this remind you of our own country?

Habakkuk was perplexed just like you and I are today. Not so much by the mixed up people we live with as by the perception that God doesn't seem to care. In Habakkuk's day those who disregarded God's law and chose to do what was right in their own eyes seemed to be doing just fine. They were rich, healthy, and happy, enjoying close-knit families and good reputations. But the good people, the faithful followers of God, the keepers of the covenant, were suffering, dealing with all sorts of problems.

Life becomes a slippery slope when we take our eyes off God and start looking at other people, comparing our circumstances to theirs, thinking that life is unfair.

So how do we deal with the perplexities of life? Do we handle it like Habakkuk did? When he found himself face-down, helpless and confused, he looked up. And in the presence of God, he didn't hold back the questions that troubled him. He dared ask, "How long, O LORD, must I call for help, but you do not listen? Or cry out to you . . . , but you do not save?" (Hab. 1:2).

When you face the dilemmas of life, when your mind is pounded with hard questions, do you ask God about it? Why not? Are you afraid you will offend him? Do you hesitate to ask because you don't think he has an answer? Are you afraid you can't handle the truth? Do you think you won't be able to understand it, so you just don't ask? Do you fear the answer might distort your view of God?

Our enemy is always trying to destroy our confidence in the goodness of God. Have you ever had your faith falter because of a question like this: "You don't believe that a good God—a kind, loving God—would permit that, do you?" Sounds like the question the tempter asked Eve in the Garden of Eden, doesn't it? "You don't think God really meant to say no to that, do you? It's just a piece of fruit. You can have it if you want; after all, God wants you to be wise." Our lives today would be so different if Eve had simply gone to God and asked the right questions.

---

*F*aith is believing what God says
simply because it is God who said it.

John Wesley

Several years ago, our beloved pastor, Bob Hamilton, was diagnosed with an inoperable brain tumor. Within a year he died. Before his death, he preached a series of sermons on heaven. The messages seemed to help the church through the long, difficult grieving process. In one of his last messages, he leaned over the pulpit, trying to make eye contact, wanting to ease our distress. Many of us were fighting back tears. He must have noticed. He took a deep breath, then, with amazing strength in his voice, declared, "God is good!" Not getting the response he wanted, he stood on tiptoes and added, "He is!" At that, the congregation gave a rather subdued but heartfelt "*Ahhmen!*"

For as long as he lived, our pastor never stopped believing, never stopped preaching, the truth that "God is good!" In spite of his impending death, the goodness of God was his deep-settled conviction. And it became the church's heart cry. At his funeral I remembered that "God is good" even though losing my pastor didn't feel good at all.

Habakkuk set the right example for us. He had questions and he took them to God. He asked the same kind of questions you and I ask as we grapple with tough issues. Why do the wicked prosper and the righteous suffer? Why doesn't God do something? Why does he allow evil among his own people? When will the suffering end? God doesn't mind our questions, in fact he invites them. When we are bold enough to come to him and ask, answers come and our faith grows. God answered Habakkuk. In essence he said, "I am working, but if I told you what I'm doing, you wouldn't believe it." Now here's the rub. He was going to use the Babylonians, a nation in worse spiritual condition than Israel, a blatantly wicked nation, to correct his own people.

Unbelievable!

Isn't that the way it is? You ask God to solve some problem for you and then hate the solution he gives. We pray and prescribe our own answers. We want God to do it our way, to do one certain thing. But God's ways are mysterious. We often misunderstand. When he begins to work, we find ourselves thinking, *Not that! Not that way!* But the truth is, God often uses strange incidents, unbelievable circumstances, ungodly people, even sin to accomplish his purposes. That's what happened in Habakkuk's day, and in the whole confusing process the prophet learned something about living in faith.

Habakkuk started seeing things God's way. He quit trying to figure things out, forgot for a moment the immediate problem, and focused instead on something he was sure about—the nature and character of God. He calls him "my God, my Holy One . . . O Rock" (1:12)—names that indicate God's presence, his power, his steadfastness. Because he knows God is always present and never changes, Habakkuk bows in reverence and proclaims, "O LORD, are you not from everlasting?" (1:12).

When our three sons were teens, we had our share of faith-testing experiences. One evening near midnight our son Mike called. (Don't you hate having the phone ring in the middle of the night? It usually means trouble of some kind!) Anyway, Mike's voice shook as he reported, "Dad, my car wouldn't start so I opened the hood and started jiggling cables. You're not going to believe this, but my battery blew up! Right in my face. It spewed junk all over my clothes. You've got to come get me."

Joe cleared his throat and wiped sleep from his eyes. At least Mike was alive and able to speak, though what he was saying didn't make much sense. Joe pulled on a pair of jeans and started toward the door. He looked back over his shoulder and quipped, "I don't know anything worse than having teenage sons driving around town in cars!" Then he apparently remembered a similar incident our friends recently had with one of their teens. He grinned and added, "Unless it's having a girl riding around in a car."

An hour or so later Mike poked his head into the bedroom to let me know he was okay. His jeans were full of holes from the battery acid, but his cute face wasn't scarred. (I'm his mom, I can think he's cute if I want to!) The above incident was one of the minor ones we had to deal with during our sons' high school and college years. Those were the days I learned to pray in faith.

Almost every morning I took a long walk down the country road near our house, and while I walked, I prayed for our kids. At first I tried to imagine all the possible scenarios they might encounter that day. I tried to cover all the bases as I petitioned God. Then one day I had an "Aha!" moment, and my prayer life changed dramatically. I didn't stop praying specifically for the situations I knew my children would face, but I added something that lifted my thoughts to a higher plane. I began talking to God about his character, his attributes, his nature. My prayers went something like this: "God, I believe you are sovereign so nothing can happen today outside your control. Heavenly Father, you are love. Thank you for loving my children more than I do. I know that you are good, so I believe everything that happens today will ultimately be for the good of my kids. You are just and fair and trustworthy, and so I will trust you. I will hang on to what I believe about you no matter what happens."

Usually by the time I got back home and unlaced my tennis shoes, my heart was full of peace and grace. I was ready to face the challenges and blessings of each day with confidence. There's nothing more consoling when we're pressed by problems and wondering what's going to happen next than to remember that God is outside this realm. His throne is above the world and outside of time. He is the everlasting God.

Habakkuk's feet were firmly planted on the solid ground of truth because he had heard from God. Can you remember a time when you heard from God? Perhaps the word of truth came as you read the Bible.[2] Maybe God spoke through a concerned friend or a professional counselor. But however the truth broke through to you, it became a rock beneath your feet. Truth is like that. Frustration fades and faith grows when God speaks.

Habakkuk questioned God, listened to him, and responded in faith. Then he went further. "I will stand at my watch and station myself on the ramparts: I will look to see what he will say to me" (Hab. 2:1). It is not enough just to pray, to tell God about our problems; we must "look." The word means much more than a casual glance. It describes a watchful waiting. The word actually means "to lean forward," "to observe." To "look," to "wait expectantly," is important for us just as it was for Habakkuk.

Our youngest grandson, Myles, taught us all an important lesson in watchful waiting one summer when the youngster was playing baseball. As our son Mike coached the team he gave each child a chance to play the different positions. One afternoon it was Myles's turn to be catcher. Mike helped him put on his gear—a bulky chest protector and cup, shin guards that dragged in the dirt as he walked, and an oversized face mask. With his cap turned backward and a huge mitt on his hand, he was ready to play ball.

Myles had no sooner squatted behind home plate than the pitching machine began hurling balls his direction. Mike said that every ball whizzed past the little guy's face on one side or the other and rattled the chain-link backstop behind him.

Mike called a time-out, put his arm around Myles's shoulder, and whispered in his ear, "Son, you look good out here. But, well, why don't you try to catch the ball?"

Myles pushed back his mask, looked up at Mike, and said, "I can't catch the ball, Daddy. I got my eyes closed."

Now, I ask you, isn't that like some of us adults? We've got our gear on—the full armor of God. We may even be in the right place at the right time. But we're just not looking. And the fastballs of life are whizzing past us, filling our hearts with fear. There's a whole bunch of us women who need to keep our eye on the ball. We need to "look" expectantly like Habakkuk did, "to see what he will say to me." When we see him and hear him well, then we can respond in faith.

Great faith means little fear; great fear means little faith.

The Upside-Down Truth...

While Habakkuk was waiting, he made a clear-cut, well-thought-out decision: "I will stand." He gave a vivid word picture when he said he would "station" himself on "the ramparts" or "watchtower" (NLT). It really means I will "set myself" there or I will "stay."

Have you ever seen a watchtower?

Recently my husband and I visited an inmate in a nearby Texas prison. As we drove through the gates, I noticed a tower near the parking lot. From the guard's vantage point inside, he could watch the prisoners playing basketball on a distant court as well as all the comings and goings in the parking lot. He had a clear view of the perimeter with its protective fence topped with razor wire. I felt safe having the guard positioned there, keeping watch.

Spiritually speaking, Habakkuk's vantage point high above earth's playing field gave him a different perspective too. By seeing life from this point of view, he began to understand what God was doing. And he was able to release all his frustration and fear into the hands of his heavenly Father.

Once Habakkuk took a stand, after he decided to wait, he expected an answer. Once we have given our problem to God, we should cease to worry about it, take our eyes off the problem, and gaze upon God. Amazingly, it is at this point that I sometimes fail. Even after I've prayed, after I've seen the problem from God's perspective, I have trouble leaving it with him. Can you identify with me? Do you pick up your problems and worry about them again? Habakkuk was determined. He said, in effect, "I'm going to get out of the vale of depression, I am going to the heights, I am going to stay put, and I'm going to keep on looking until I hear from God."

Four steps from the pen of Habakkuk define his exercise in faith.

Habakkuk's Faith-ercise

"I will stand."

"I will stay."

"I will look."

"He will speak."

Because of Habakkuk's faith—a belief well-established by his own statements of faith and based upon the revealed, personal word of God—he was able to endure when his land was invaded by the Babylonians. He survived when many of Israel's brightest and best young men (including Daniel and his three friends) were taken captive. He trusted God, believing in what he had said, standing on what he had promised. He believed what he could not prove because he trusted the one who said it. Habakkuk went on to record for our encouragement some of the most noteworthy insights on faith ever recorded in Scripture. Again he was following God's direction. "Write the vision and make it plain" (Hab. 2:2 NKJV).

And so he wrote: "The just shall live by his faith" (Hab. 2:4 NKJV). The verse is repeated three times in Scripture: to show the difference between Christian beliefs and those of the pagan world,[3] to contrast the faith-life with living under the law,[4] and to give confidence to believers in the face of suffering and persecutions.[5] Kay Arthur claims, "This verse is the key to all of life. The key to the whole Word of God."[6] When Martin Luther discovered this verse and really understood the depth of its message, he realized the truth of the gospel—salvation was for those who believed, an act of mercy not merit. The truth sparked the Reformation, which changed the whole direction of the Christian church.

Habakkuk also penned the magnificent words that have been sung by choirs and congregations throughout the centuries of Christendom—the church's great doxology, our call to worship. The words express our feelings when we come to a place where there's nothing more to say, no more arguments or questions worth asking. "The LORD is in His holy temple. Let all the earth keep silence before Him" (Hab. 2:20 NKJV).

He wrote these words that help us face the future with hope. "The earth will be filled with the knowledge of the glory of the LORD, as the waters cover the sea" (Hab. 2:14).

The final words that he wrote have become a statement of faith for struggling women like you and me. No matter what devastation may come our way, we can stand firm if we adopt Habakkuk's attitude. "Though the fig tree may not blossom, nor fruit be on the vines; though the labor of the olive may fail, and the fields yield no food; though the flock may be cut off from the fold, and there be no herd in the stalls—yet I will rejoice in the LORD, I will joy in the God of my salvation" (Hab. 3:17–18 NKJV).

Following this declaration Habakkuk remembers God's faithfulness in the past, and is able to fully trust him in present daily situations. His gaze turned from God above to his own feet firmly planted on the earth. "The LORD God is my strength; He will make my feet like deer's feet, and He will make me walk on my high hills" (Hab. 3:19 NKJV).

In all of life's uncertainties, with our doubts and fears, in sticky situations (even those of our own making), when unexplainable things happen, God is always faithful. He will make our feet like the feet of a deer so we can dance on high places, keeping step with the happy feet of Habakkuk.

Right-Side Up

1. Read chapter 11 of Hebrews. Who are some of the characters who lived by faith? Describe what happened. Why do you think their names were listed in Faith's Hall of Fame?

2. Read Hebrews 11:6. What does this verse teach? Why is faith so important?

3. When Habakkuk said, "We will not die," he was remembering God's covenant. He knew God had a plan for Israel and they would not be wiped out. What does God's covenant mean to you personally?

4. What is the promise of Deuteronomy 33:27?

5. In the Amplified Version of the New Testament, Hebrews 13:5 reads:

   I will not in any way fail you nor give you up nor leave you without support. [I will] not, [I will] not, [I will] not in any degree leave you helpless nor forsake nor let [you] down (relax My hold on you)! [Assuredly not!]

   Did you notice the three "I wills"? What does this promise mean to you? How does it make you feel?

6. What does Romans 14:23 say to us today?

7. Romans 10:17 tells us how to acquire more faith. What is the solution to a lack of faith?

8. What kind of attitude does Psalm 5:3 encourage?

9. Read Psalm 62:1, 5–8. Discuss these thoughts with your group or meditate upon them in your own time alone with God.

10

Working Out What God Works In

Discovering What Salvation Requires

Work out your salvation with fear and trembling, for it is God who works in you to will and to act according to his good purpose.

Philippians 2:12–13

If salvation is a gift of God's grace and completely free, then why does this verse say we must work it out? We're told not only to work but to do so with fear and trembling. That sounds serious . . . and hard! On the other hand, the verse says it is God who's doing the work—accomplishing his purposes in our lives from the inside out (or from the upside down). Since our all-powerful God is busy working out his plan on our behalf, then why do we have to do anything at all? This kind of thinking is confusing to most of us, but we can take comfort that we're not the first to wonder about it.

The disciples needed clarification as well. They asked, "What must we do to do the works God requires?" Jesus answered, "The work of God is this: to believe in the one he has sent" (John 6:28–29). That sounds easy enough—until you come across other verses about salvation that add obedience and discipline to the mix. When such apparent contradictions are expressed in the Bible, no wonder it throws us off balance.

So what am I supposed to do?

Let's understand from the start, "work out your salvation" does not suggest work *for* your salvation. We've been told clearly that salvation is "not by works of righteousness which we have done" (Titus 3:5 NKJV); it is "by grace . . . not by works" (Eph. 2:8–9). Besides that, the instruction in Philippians is written to the "saints"[1]—to women like you and me who have believed in Christ. Author Warren Wiersbe explains: "'Work out' means 'work to full completion,' such as working out a problem in mathematics." He claims the phrase was also used for "working a mine" to retrieve all the valuable ore or "working a field" to gather in a great harvest. "The purpose God wants us to achieve is Christlikeness, 'to be conformed to the image of His Son.' There are problems in life, but God will help us to 'work them out.' Our lives have tremendous potential, like a mine or a field, and He wants to help us fulfill that potential."[2]

Realizing your full potential includes finding your own way, discovering the path you are destined to walk upon. Words penned by the apostle Paul reveal that a divine plan has been laid out for all of us, a life plan that includes far more than our first step of faith. We tend to forget that immediately following his bold declaration that salvation comes "not as a result of works," he tells us that we are "created in Christ Jesus for good works, which God prepared beforehand" (Eph. 2:10 NASB). After we have been saved "by grace," it's important that we discover exactly what God created us to do, then do precisely that. What we are really talking about is finding our purpose in life, and it includes figuring out our distinctive personality traits; our spiritual gifts; our God-given interests, goals, and desires. The process may be one of fits and starts as we work it out, and it will probably include making a few wrong turns or even getting lost for a while as we trip along, trying to find the right pathway. Such was the experience of our youngest son, Jason.

While attending college, he took a giant step in working out his own salvation when he made a U-turn on his career path. For many years he'd said he wanted to be a counselor. I liked the idea. Since I was involved in mentoring women, I often ended up helping people with family and personal problems. It seemed a compliment to me that my son wanted to walk in his mom's footsteps. So I bought books for us to share, and we had long talks about people problems and their biblical solutions. I also noticed qualities in Jason's life that would help him in a counseling ministry. He was a good listener, and at times I was amazed at his suggested solutions to some of life's struggles.

Then after his second year of college, Jason told me something important. He'd changed his mind about becoming a counselor. At first I was a bit disappointed. But I knew then as I do now that God has a plan for every life. It's an individual matter that nobody else can discover for another person—not even a mother for her child. Jason's life could have become one big mess if he had ended up doing what his mom thought he should do instead of what God called him to do. (Yikes! Maybe there's a bunch of us moms who need to get out of the way and let our kids work out their own salvation.) As it has turned out, I was right about Jason's qualifications for people-helping. He's top man on his human resources team helping people find a suitable job and taking care of job-related problems that come up along the way. Even though he is not in a church-related vocation, Jason is definitely "called" to do what he does. He is working out his own salvation one day at a time.

This kind of spiritual work may also mean equipping yourself through education and training. My friend Cynthia got two master's degrees on her path toward becoming a Christian counselor. For seven years she worked, using her training and her spiritual gifts in a well-known counseling center in Dallas. Then she got married and became a mom. Today she is living out a new phase of life as she cares for three incredible kids, ministers to her husband, and works in her flower gardens. Now I ask you, is it more important for Cynthia to work in an office with her colleagues or in her home with her family? Which is more spiritual, more God-centered, more in line with his will and purpose?

Cynthia says, "Every phase of my life is equally important as I seek God's will for each day. Whether I am speaking to a large group of women or deadheading in my flower beds I am working out my own salvation with 'fear and trembling,' trying to follow the leadership of God and the verse that tells me, 'Whatever you do in word or deed, do all in the name of the Lord Jesus'" (Col. 3:17 NASB).

Is Cynthia still using her training and spiritual gifts? Absolutely! She is an author and an inspirational speaker who travels throughout the United States bringing hope and encouragement to women.[3] She's active in her church and the community where she lives. Besides that, whenever I need a word of kindness or advice, Cynthia is just a phone call away. Believe me, knowing there's a sympathetic counselor hanging around in my cellular phone space feels really good to me. So I'm glad Cynthia is exactly where she is right now, doing her God-appointed work and showing the rest of us what following on to know the Lord really means.[4]

Seems to me we make this whole idea of "working it out" harder than it has to be. Don't forget that in the very same sentence where we're told to "work," we're told that "it is God who works," and he's doing it in a way that's beyond our human ability. While we are working on things from the outside in, he works from the inside out. The verse says, "Both to will and to act according to his good purpose" (Phil. 2:13). An older translation, but one we may be more familiar with, says that God is working in us "to will and to do" (KJV). That means he is working on our will, changing our hearts, motivating us from within; then, when we come to a place where we want what he wants, he gives us the ability to do it. We find that we have all the power, strength, determination, and grace needed to put into practice, to follow through with, whatever plan and purpose he's already put within our soul. Does that make sense?

It's easy for me to relax in my walk with Christ when I read these words from an easier-to-understand translation. "Be energetic in your life of salvation, reverent and sensitive before God. That energy is God's energy, an energy deep within you, God himself willing and working at what will give him the most pleasure" (Phil. 2:12–13 Message). Do you get what he's saying here? Our part is to be "sensitive before God," open and responsive to what he is saying, to how he is leading. God's part is to reveal, inspire, energize, give clear direction, and open doors of opportunity. Jesus has not left us to our own resources but is himself providing everything we need to do the things that bring him pleasure. Our faith begins and ends in him.

Looking unto Jesus, the author and finisher of our faith.

Hebrews 12:2 KJV

Probably nobody has exhibited this kind of faith experience better than Saul of Tarsus. Do you remember what happened to him? Nobody would argue this man was saved by God's grace.[5] And what an unworthy recipient! The New Testament describes a tyrant who burst into the homes of Christians, torturing them and hauling them off to jail.[6] In fact, Saul's before-salvation purpose was to destroy this ragtag group of radicals who had upset the Jewish establishment.[7]

Before Saul met Jesus, he was making a name for himself in Judaism, a spiritual leader who was moving up in the ranks. According to his own testimony, he "was extremely zealous for the traditions of [his] fathers" (Gal. 1:14). Then Jesus came to him in a brilliant flash of light that knocked his feet from under him and made him temporarily blind. Even though he couldn't see a thing, Saul did not remain in the dark about who had interrupted his self-directed life. Almost immediately, he calls him "Lord," a term that means much more than "savior." Saul was acknowledging and bowing to his new Master. And he'd no sooner caught his breath than he asked a question—a question that every true believer in Jesus will ask: "What do You want me to do?" (Acts 9:6 NKJV).

During the following days, when he could see nothing, physically speaking that is, Saul (who would later be known as Paul) received remarkable spiritual insight. He was baptized, filled with the Holy Spirit, and couldn't wait to tell the people of Damascus what had happened to him. Before long he would retreat to a place of solitude.

Years later when he wrote his first message—the letter to the Galatians—Paul let us know how he discovered his purpose. It's important to note that he did not confer with anyone else, not even the disciples. Instead, he headed into the desert to be alone with God. For three years he listened and prayed, and when he emerged from Arabia, he knew what God wanted him to do. He would take the message of Christ to the Gentiles. From that point on, as he worked out his salvation, no matter what obstacles he faced, he never wavered from his calling. He knew who he was and where he was going. You can almost hear the confident tone in the written words: "Paul, an apostle—sent not from men nor by man, but by Jesus Christ and God the Father, who raised him from the dead" (Gal. 1:1). Later he added, "The gospel which was preached by me is not according to man. For I neither received it from man, nor was I taught it, but I received it through a revelation of Jesus Christ" (Gal. 1:11–12 NASB).

Chances are most of us won't have such a dramatic experience with Jesus, but he does come to us, making his claim on our lives. And when he does, we will not need to consult with anybody else—not Mom and Dad or the pastor of our local church. God will reveal his will to every seeking heart in his own time in his own way. He may give you a completely new life-direction like he did for Paul. He may give you a simple midcourse correction (especially if you believe when you are a child). To others he may give a temporary assignment, one that may last a few months or a few years before he sends you in a different direction.

But he will definitely give you light for the next step on the path every day of your life. He does this through his Word and by the leadership of the Holy Spirit.

My friend Kara trusted Christ as her Savior when she was twelve. Even though she was a young girl, she immediately wanted to obey the Lord. She said, "There was a new desire in me, a longing to be different, to change some of my behavior patterns." She wanted to be baptized and started thinking about making a difference in the world. Kara began reading the Bible, establishing a pattern she still follows today as she cares for her husband and their two preschool daughters.

"The Bible is very important to me," Kara said. "It's the way to know God, and it is my instruction booklet on how to live. In my opinion, faith is not a sit-on-the-sidelines kind of thing, it's active."

Kara barely finished that last sentence when her four-year-old daughter, Grace, who had apparently been listening in on our conversation, popped through the doorway and, like a pint-sized cheerleader, yelled, "It's get-up-and-go."

Kara and I burst out laughing. Tidy little summation of what we'd been saying, huh? After we'd gained our composure, Kara continued. "I know that salvation is a gift of God's grace. But when someone you love gives you a present, you don't accept it and then turn your back on the one who gave it to you. You want them to see you enjoying the gift, you want to share the joy. To me that's what the Bible means when it

> Faith alone saves, but the faith that saves is not alone.
>
> John Calvin

The Upside-Down Truth...

says 'faith without works is dead.'[8] You just can't have one without the other."

The author of Colossians made the whole faith/works concept simple for us when he wrote, "Just as you received Christ Jesus as Lord, continue to live in him" (Col. 2:6). How did you receive Jesus? By faith? By finally grasping the reality of who he is, accepting his love, allowing him to free you from the sin burden you had been carrying? Did he come into the very heart of your life, bringing to you a sense of peace and freedom? Were you aware of a divine presence afterward? If that is how you "received Christ Jesus the Lord," then continue in the same pattern every day of your life one step at a time. It is a life of trusting, accepting, receiving his grace, obeying the truth as we see it, following in his steps. While it is true that you receive salvation freely with no strings attached, it is also true that from that first moment of faith your life is not your own.[9]

"We are God's workmanship" (Eph. 2:10)—God's "handiwork" or "poem." Now, those are two words I can get my mind around. Handiwork, like a piece of fabric embroidered one creative stitch at a time, or a poem that an author composes line upon line. We ourselves are God's "work," and he is in the process of completing what he has begun.[10] While God is working, we are to cooperate by staying stretched on the loom or by holding still so he can write his message on our hearts. In other words, our "work" is allowing him to work, submitting to his hand, arriving at a place of quiet trust where we are willing to accept whatever happens and believe there is good in it. It is also up to us to put ourselves in a place where we can grow.[11] That includes spending time with God, getting to know him, allowing him to show us his plan, to mold us, change our hearts, give direction.

Peter encourages us to grow in eight specific areas: "Make every effort to add to your faith goodness; and to goodness, knowledge; and to knowledge, self-control; and to self-control, perseverance; and to perseverance, godliness; and to godliness, brotherly kindness; and to brotherly kindness, love" (2 Peter 1:5–7). Don't skip over the part of the verse that says to "make every effort." These qualities will not just pop up in our lives because we are Christians. It takes diligence on our part to make sure these things come together, like a skilled choreographer puts together the various aspects of a chorus or play.

Recently the magnificent movie *The Sound of Music* celebrated its fortieth anniversary. Not many films enjoy the status or endure the test of time like this classic. Why has this production remained popular for so long? For one thing, it is the story of a family with all the mystique and love and humor that comes when a single man is trying to raise seven children. It might help that he is incredibly handsome and falls in love with the children's governess. The intrigue of living in Austria during the Second World War adds to the drama. But I think *The Sound of Music* has endured because of its splendid choreography and the music of Rodgers and Hammerstein. Do you remember the opening scene? Cameras pan the majestic cliffs and crags of Austria's Alps. Puffy white clouds dot the clear blue skies where birds dip and soar. The sight alone is breathtaking. Then the music begins and crescendos, filling the canyons and bouncing off the face of the mountain. Suddenly a wisp of a girl, the fresh-faced Julie Andrews, pops into the scene. With arms outstretched she whirls and swoops and bursts into song: "The hills are alive with the sound of music." Makes my heart skip a beat just thinking about it!

Not until the release of the fortieth anniversary edition of the musical did I find out something interesting. In a series of outtakes, Julie Andrews revealed a few glitches that occurred on that grassy hillside nestled between the jagged peaks. For one thing, the helicopter hovering overhead to shoot the pictures circled too closely at times. The wind off the whirring propeller would completely knock Miss Andrews off her feet, sending her sprawling. She'd jump up, dust herself off, and try again. The whole ordeal became a comedy of miscommunication as she'd wave frantically, trying to get the pilot to move away. Thinking she was enthusiastic about the take, he'd give a thumbs-up and circle around again. Apparently the hills were alive that day with a lot more than the sound of music. But you know what? In spite of Miss Andrews's bumps and bruises, the scene got filmed and the results are history.

Is that what Peter was trying to communicate to us when he wrote about the growth of certain Christian graces in our lives? He is not talking about simply adding one virtue to the next but rather the development of one quality in the exercise of another, each grace springing out of the one before. For example, in your faith, as you cling to what you believe, goodness or moral excellence develops. In goodness, knowledge grows. As you advance in knowledge, self-control springs forth; and in self-control, perseverance increases. As you develop more grace to abide under difficult or stressful circumstances, godliness is produced. Alongside godliness comes brotherly kindness, and with brotherly kindness, love. Perhaps as our salvation is "worked out," these graces will eventually fit together in our lives, creating vibrant harmony like a well-choreographed drama. Then we will rejoice in the reality of this promise: "For if you possess these qualities in increasing measure, they will keep you from being ineffective and unproductive in your knowledge of our Lord Jesus Christ" (2 Peter 1:8).

So does "working out your salvation" mean being more disciplined? Maybe, maybe not! I know one thing for sure: Without discipline we will never find time for prayer. If there's no structure in our lives, there will be no Bible study. And without that kind of nourishment, there will be no spiritual growth, no development toward Christlikeness.[12] On the other hand, I've known some women who are very disciplined, but they don't seem one bit more Christlike than their undisciplined counterparts. Makes me wonder if they got caught up in some method, some routine, and missed the message. I wonder if they have focused more on learning stuff about God and forgot that the Christian life is about having a relationship with him.

A woman I'll call Jan loved to do her Bible study lesson. She carefully marked the text with different colors and symbols. After she colored all the key words, she would make lists—very complete and detailed lists—including everything the chapter said about God, about Jesus, about certain important words. Every blank space in her workbook was filled in, every question answered.

As leader of the group, I couldn't help but be impressed. But then I began to notice something troubling. Jan seemed to lack a few of the Christian graces I'd come to expect in a woman so well taught. She seemed perturbed at the inefficiency of some of the others in the group. She became frustrated and detached. I started wondering what was wrong. I wondered how I could help her connect, how to steer her in a better direction. So I decided to reemphasize something important. We're not only to observe the text (the part Jan enjoyed immensely), but we're also to interpret it and, most importantly, allow the Holy Spirit to apply the truth to our everyday lives. If we "abide" in him and his Word "abides" in us (John 15:7 NASB), if we let the Word of Christ "dwell" in us richly (Col. 3:16), our hearts will be changed, and we'll become softer, gentler Christians, women who know Christ better and who love each other more.

Can you understand or maybe even identify with Jan? Seems to me it's easy to miss the mark when it comes to the Christian disciplines, especially if you are of the studious sort—if you like notebooks and lists and memory verse cards. Besides that, all of us are engaged in a spiritual battle, a battle for our minds. If our adversary can't trip us up one way, he'll make us stumble in another. I don't mind admitting that there are times, even in my most spiritual moments, when I have to remind myself to slow down, think about what I'm reading, and give God time to speak to my heart. I am so thankful for the many different programs and methods I've used through the years to help me get into God's Word (and that have helped God's Word get into me). But let's not forget that studying the Bible is not an end in itself. The purpose is to know Christ better, not only as your Lord, but as the friend and lover of your soul. It's the whole thing!

As we concentrate on working out our salvation, maybe we need to simply become more yielded, more submissive to God, more open to his Spirit, and more aware of his grace. Maybe we need to become better listeners and better responders, rather than better disciplined and more organized. I know thoughts like these are a lot harder to get our minds around than some new Bible study technique. It's easier to buy a notebook, find some colored pencils, and get going. But for those of you who might be wanting something more, why not walk down a new pathway? Begin by asking God to reveal to you the magnitude of your salvation.

Have you ever been stopped dead in your tracks by the thought of what happened on Calvary? Has it taken your breath away, made your heart beat faster? Do you live in the knowledge that one moment in time changed your life forever?

Ask God to show you exactly what happened on the cross. Ask him to show you what he is doing about your salvation right now, today. The results of that kind of query will be heartwarming, life changing, and real.

My friend Julie experienced this recently at a women's conference. The event coordinator had asked if she would like to participate in a communion service. Of course Julie said yes. As she stood at the front of the conference center, holding a broken loaf of bread in her hands, the women filed by one by one, each breaking off a tiny piece of the loaf. Julie said, "Suddenly, I was overcome. I wanted to say, 'This is his body, which was broken for you,' but I couldn't speak. I thought about how broken Jesus was as he hung there on the cross and that he did it for me. In a moment of reality I knew how broken I was, how broken all of us are." Her emotions soaring, Julie swallowed hard, trying to hold back the tears pooling in her eyes, to keep her chin from quivering. She prayed silently, hoping the women parading by would understand. But even that didn't really matter as her heart was focused on Jesus. "I don't know what made that communion service different from many others I have observed, but it changed my life. I will never be the same."

These grand moments of faith happen only occasionally in our lives, but when they do, we get a glimpse of how much salvation costs, of how deserving Jesus is to have our whole hearts and lives. Perhaps that's how we work the rich ore from the deep gold mine we call salvation.

ℛight-Side Up

1. At one time or another, Jesus asks all of us the question he asked Peter: "Will you lay down your life for My sake?" (John 13:38 NKJV). Can you remember a time when he asked this of you? Read 1 John 3:16. What do these words mean to you personally?

2. First Corinthians 6:19 states, "You are not your own." What does that verse mean? What does it mean to you? Do you remember the first time you realized this truth?

3. Read John 14:15. What helps us obey the commandments of Jesus?

4. Colossians 3:23–24 gives us much-needed insight into our "work" for God. Read the verses and answer the five questions, Who? What? When? Why? and How?

5. What does Romans 12:1–2 teach?

6. Galatians 5:22–23 lists nine character qualities that most of us want to see developing in our lives. The "fruit of the Spirit" will be obvious in the life of every Christian who is "working out" her salvation. List the kinds of fruit and examine yourself.

Are these qualities present? Are they developing into stronger traits?

7. What can we do to make the fruit grow? Galatians 5:25 gives us a clue. What does the verse say?

8. Read 2 Corinthians 2:14–15. What kind of work should we do? Is this verse more about "being" or "doing"?

9. What does James 1:22 teach?

10. Salvation is a process. It is described as
    • a race (1 Cor. 9:24–27)
    • a pursuit (Rom. 14:19 NASB)
    • a contest (Phil. 3:12–14)
    • a fight (1 Tim. 6:12)

    Read the verses that use these analogies. Do these word pictures describe your life? Why or why not?

❧ 11 ❧

Maturing into Childhood

Understanding the Process
of Growing Up Spiritually

Whoever humbles himself like this child is the greatest in
the kingdom of heaven.

Matthew 18:4

When the disciples came to Jesus and asked, "Who is the
greatest in the kingdom of heaven?" (Matt. 18:1), he called
a child and had him stand among them. Then he said something that must have turned their minds upside down.
"Unless you change and become like little children, you
will never enter the kingdom of heaven" (v. 3).

This kind of thinking is more than a little confusing to
women like you and me. We value maturity, education,
and experience. We tend to think we can't get a handle on

spiritual matters without these assets. But Jesus is saying just the opposite, not only to the original twelve, but to those of us who are following him today. He's not looking for disciples whom the world considers great or important. He doesn't take into account a person's credentials—a college degree or prestigious position in society. Instead, he tells us we must become like a child.

In the Gospel of Mark, we are given more insight into Jesus's point of view on children. A group of parents brought their children to Jesus, wanting him to touch them. The disciples failed to see the value in such activity. They were focused on "more important" things, like how to usher in the eternal kingdom. To them these children seemed a nuisance, disrupting their plans and distracting Jesus from his "real" purpose. Taking matters into their own hands, the disciples told those parents to step back. It must have created an awkward situation for the parents and embarrassed the precious children as well. Jesus was incensed! "Let the little children come to me, and do not hinder them, for the kingdom of God belongs to such as these. I tell you the truth, anyone who will not receive the kingdom of God like a little child will never enter it" (Mark 10:14–15). Then Jesus took the children in his arms, placed his hands on them, and blessed them.

To say that Jesus loves children seems a great understatement. He loves them so much that he identifies with them, taking upon himself the lack of respect, the sting of rejection, they must feel anytime they are mistreated. In fact, Matthew 18:6 contains one of the strongest warnings in Scripture: "Whoever causes one of these little ones who believe in Me to stumble, it would be better for him to have a heavy millstone hung around his neck, and to be drowned in the depth of the sea" (NASB). And when a child is treated well, Jesus nods in approval.

*W*hoever welcomes a little child like this
in my name welcomes me.

Matthew 18:5

If we knew what age child Jesus had placed into that circle of seasoned disciples, it would help us know the qualities he wants us to emulate. Was Jesus looking into the face of a toddler or a preschooler? If he was, chances are the child was one who had not been wounded by some of the life-altering experiences we grown-ups have had to face. The child on his lap was full of grace and joy. A child with dreams and hope for the future.

The aging apostle John gave us some insight into this when he wrote his first epistle. He often called his converts "little children." It puts a smile on my face to think about this grandfatherly man referring to his spiritual descendants as children. Not all of them were young, but all of them began as spiritual babes and were growing in the faith.

> I am writing to you, little children, because your sins have been forgiven you for His name's sake. I am writing to you, fathers, because you know Him who has been from the beginning. I am writing to you, young men, because you have overcome the evil one. I have written to you, children, because you know the Father. I have written to you, fathers, because you know Him who has been from the beginning. I have written to you, young men, because you are strong, and the word of God abides in you, and you have overcome the evil one.
>
> 1 John 2:12–14 NASB

Did you notice the different groups he mentioned? "Little children," "fathers," "children," "young men." Each term designates a stage of growth and comes from a unique Greek word. One of the words John chose means "darlings." He used that term to describe the phase of a child's development that comes after infancy, before "childhood." I'm thinking, maybe three to five years old. Have you ever referred to one of your own children or grandchildren as your "little darling"? It's a term of endearment that speaks of innocence, freedom, spontaneity, and grace—characteristics typical of this age group. I can't help but think it was one of the "darlings" in the crowd whom Jesus reached for, pulling her onto his lap for a hug and a bit of conversation. In doing so, he was showing his life-hardened disciples an important truth. It's a message we women need to hear as well. If we want to be a part of Jesus's kingdom, we must become one of his "darlings."

"Unless you become like a child . . ." The whole idea got me thinking about what that would entail. Why would Jesus tell grown-up women like you and me, with all our training and experience, to go back in time? What exactly does it mean? Is it even possible to do? The more I thought about it, the more I realized what a profound statement Jesus made on that occasion. He not only laid out the path toward a blessed life but warned us of the major pitfalls we might encounter along the way.

For one thing, being childlike means having genuine humility. When Matthew recorded the story of Jesus and the children, he basically said that we grown-ups will never come to know Christ unless we somehow find the humility of a child. "I assure you, unless you turn from your sins and become as little children, you will never get into the Kingdom of Heaven. Therefore, anyone who becomes as humble as this little child is the greatest in the Kingdom of Heaven" (Matt. 18:3–4 NLT).

It is pride that keeps many adults from accepting the grace of God. It is much easier for us grown-ups to give and to serve others in sacrificial ways than it is to simply come and receive a gift. There's a certain kind of pride that moves some people to give their lives in humanitarian causes. But receiving the gift of salvation means we have to admit we are sinners, powerless to help ourselves, having no ability to earn or win a place in God's kingdom. Until we realize we are absolutely destitute and completely lost, Jesus cannot help us. And so he waits for each of us to come to a place of childlike humility, a place where we give up our independence, stop all self-effort, and accept his free gift.[1]

Children find it easy to depend upon God. They come into the world totally dependent. They can't eat, or drink, or take care of even one essential need without help from their parents or other caring adult. They rely on their mother for nourishment. They grow in emotional health as they rest in her arms, feeling her heartbeat, enjoying the fragrance of her warm breath as she whispers or sings to them. Such conditioning makes it easy for the child to nestle in the arms of God, to receive his unconditional love. When they get a little older, they are not prideful about asking for help. "Help me!" "Feed me!" "Hold me!" Infants who are well-nurtured grow into children free from the compulsion to earn or pay back God's love.

Those in the "darling" stage have total trust in what their parents say. During a recent visit with Cynthia, my professional-counselor-turned-mom friend, we talked about the social development of preschoolers. "If I had told my preschool son that Abraham Lincoln was the first president of the United States, he would have accepted it without question. When he got old enough for school and his teacher told him the first president was George Washington, he would not have believed her. In fact, he'd stand up and fight (verbally at least) for what I'd said. *'No! It was Abraham Lincoln. My mother said so!'* After all, to most kids nobody is as smart as Mom.

"After a child has experienced some of the inequities of life, after he or she has been deceived or hurt, it becomes harder for them to trust people," Cynthia said. "It is then that we begin to see children dealing with certain problems including skepticism, doubt, and fear."

Early the next morning Cynthia piled her two oldest children, Elisabeth and Christian, in the car and took them to school. Four-year-old Mary Camille decided to stay at home with me. We settled on the sofa, and I picked up a stack of books from the table behind the couch. Mary Camille moved onto my lap, covering her legs with her soft pink blanket. I brushed a strand of blond hair from her face and began to read *Good Night Moon*, then I read *The Three Little Kittens*. Afterward, I suggested we sit on the front porch and wait for her mommy to come home. While we waited, I struck up a conversation. "Mary Camille, you have a lot of books at your house. Do you like stories?"

"Yes, ma'am!"

"Well, I'm glad you do!" I pulled her close and continued, "Do you have a favorite story? A favorite book?"

Mary Camille's soft blue eyes danced as she broke into a big grin. Then she whispered a one-word answer: "Jesus."

It took a moment for me to get it. "Is your favorite story about Jesus?"

"Uh-huh." She slid off my lap and turned to face me. Folding her legs beneath her, she made a cradle of her arms and began swaying back and forth, back and forth, like she was rocking a baby. Her eyes focused on the make-believe infant in her arms. "So tiny. A tiny little baby."

Suddenly, she stopped rocking, stretched her arms toward the sky, and began wiggling all ten little fingers, twirling her hands in half circles. "And there were angels, angels all around. Lots of them." I caught my breath when I realized that, even though it was springtime, Mary Camille was remembering the Christmas story. My heart filled with joy and wonder. Why, I could almost see celestial beings dancing in the bright morning sunlight.

Then Mary Camille grew silent. I sat quietly too. Completely awestruck. *So that's what having the faith of a child means!* I leaned her direction and gave Mary Camille a hug.

Before long, gravel popped beneath the wheels of Cynthia's car as she pulled in the driveway. The enchanting moment had passed. But the memory of that conversation with one of God's little darlings lingers in my heart to this day. There are times when I'm feeling lonely or afraid and I remember the tender exchange between Mary Camille and me. At times like these I pause and look up. "Lord, help me have the faith of a child." Sometimes I feel compelled to add, "Forgive me for making things complicated, help me 'trust in you with all my heart,' forgive me for 'leaning to my own understanding'" (Prov. 3:5–6).

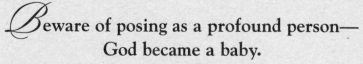

*B*eware of posing as a profound person—
God became a baby.

Oswald Chambers

Sometimes mothers think they should wait until their children are more mature before they talk to them about spiritual matters, especially when it comes to the child's salvation. When kids bring up the issue, they might ask them to wait, thinking when they're older they'll understand things better. But how much truth does a person need to know before he or she is old enough to respond in faith?

Our youngest son, Jason, was only five when he began asking questions about salvation and baptism. I answered, giving him as much spiritual info as a five-year-old could grasp (according to my humble opinion, that is). He seemed to get it, but when he asked if he could be baptized the very next Sunday, I felt uncertain. I hesitated only a few minutes before asking him to wait. I thought, *I'm not sure he's old enough to realize what Jesus really did on the cross. I don't think he gets it, when it comes to knowing the consequences of sin.* And since he'd talked mostly about baptism, I wasn't sure he was ready for the life commitment a follower of Christ must make. As I tried to explain, Jason seemed disappointed. Afterward I felt a bit confused myself. Had I done the right thing to put his faith quest on hold? Finding a quiet place, I asked God to help Jason understand, to show me what to do, and to overrule any mistakes I'd made.

Later that day, I saw my little boy walking through the pasture behind our house. He picked at the weeds, kicked at a few dirt clods, and finally settled on a circular bench his daddy had built around one of the trees in the field. Obviously the child was deep in thought. I watched him as he sat there, and I wondered what was going through his mind. Almost an hour passed before Jason wandered back inside. "Mom," he began, "I've been thinking. I do understand what happened on the cross. Jesus died for me. I asked him to come into my heart when I was sitting on that bench. I want to be baptized. Okay?"

What could I say? The truth is, I couldn't have said anything if I'd wanted to. Not until I had swallowed the lump rising in my throat. I gave him a hug and answered, "Okay! I'll call our pastor right now." Jason was baptized the following Sunday, and our family celebrated his new relationship with Jesus.

Do you think Jason was old enough to know what he was doing? Was his experience "real"? Well, he has never doubted it, not then, not twenty-some years later. Recently he brought up the subject. "Mom, do you remember when I took that long walk in our field? I didn't want you to stop me from getting things right with God. I needed to make my own decision."

I laughed before saying out loud, "Thank God for the wisdom of babes."

While some of us think it's a good thing for our children to wait until they're older, the truth is, most people come to faith in Jesus while they are very young. Almost two-thirds of the people who give their lives to Christ do so before the age of eighteen. If they don't accept Christ by the age of twenty-one, chances are they will never come to know him. When did you believe in Christ? How old were you when you were baptized? Do you still remember the event? Was it real?

One reason children come to faith early is because they accept things simply because they are. Children are not trying to be wise. They don't reason everything out or ponder all the implications of a thing like we grown-ups tend to do. These words from a modern version of the New Testament make this clear: "I'm telling you, once and for all, that unless you return to square one and start over like children, you're not even going to get a look at the kingdom, let alone get in. Whoever becomes simple and elemental again, like this child, will rank high in God's kingdom" (Matt. 18:3–4 Message). Did you notice those two key words? Simple. Elemental. Some of us need to ask forgiveness for being so complicated, so un-simple.

I have to admit there are times when I just "run things into the ground" (as my mother used to say) as I try to figure something out or work things through. I'm not saying it's wrong for me, or anyone else for that matter, to educate ourselves or want to discover something new. But there are also times when God wants us to just accept the truth. Paul warned the Corinthian believers, "I am afraid that, as the serpent deceived Eve by his craftiness, your minds will be led astray from the simplicity and purity of devotion to Christ" (2 Cor. 11:3 NASB).

Isn't it interesting that he brings up the deception of Eve? How did the serpent lead Eve away from "the simplicity of devotion to Christ"? He told her she could be like God. And she liked the idea! She questioned God's simple command not to eat the fruit of a certain tree in the garden. I think her reasoning went something like this. *Hey, all we're talking about here is a tree and a piece of fruit. Surely God didn't mean no. He probably meant not to eat it that day. On another day it might be okay. After all, God wants me to be wise.* God had said no, plain and simple. And he wanted an obedient response. When Eve started asking questions and trying to figure out why he said no, that's when she got into trouble.

"Simplicity is the secret to seeing things clearly," wrote Oswald Chambers.

In God's eyes little children are the big thing.

The Upside-Down Truth ...

"A saint does not *think* clearly until a long time passes, but a saint ought to *see* clearly without any difficulty. You cannot think through spiritual confusion to make things clear; to make things clear, you must obey. In intellectual matters you can think things out, but in spiritual matters you will only think yourself into further wandering thoughts and more confusions."[2]

If only Eve had simply obeyed! She would have saved herself a lot of pain, and alleviated a lot of trouble for future generations as well, including women like you and me. We tend to think upside down when it comes to obedience. We want to understand before we obey. But the truth is, understanding usually comes afterward. Listen again to Oswald Chambers: "If there is something in your life upon which God has put His pressure, then obey Him in that matter. Bring all your arguments and . . . 'every thought into captivity to the obedience of Christ' regarding the matter and everything will become as clear as daylight to you."[3]

Children are much more willing to see things simply, and that makes it much easier to obey. A capacity to reason things out may come later, but Mr. Chambers got it right when he added "reasoning is not how we see." We older folk who put such a high premium on wisdom need to relax and try to see like children. If we don't, we'll end up seeing nothing. While we may not understand his methods, it pleases God to reveal spiritual truth to those who will accept it in its simplest form. Jesus said, "Father . . . , you have hidden these things from the wise and learned, and revealed them to little children. Yes, Father, for this was your good pleasure" (Matt. 11:25–26).

When I was growing up, I had a no-nonsense daddy who insisted on obedience. I, being a descendant of Eve and just a tad me-centered, asked a lot of questions. Seemed to me if

Dad wanted me to do something, there had to be a reason behind it. So I usually asked. You'd think after I received the same answer over and over again, I'd stop posing questions, but I was also a bit determined. Okay, stubborn. Dad said I was just being "contrary." Anyway, when I asked why, he usually gave a simple answer. "Because I said so!"

Eventually the message got through to me. I think most of the time he didn't really have a reason. (Do you remember ever telling your kids no because, even though you couldn't give a reason, you had an uneasy feeling, an unexplainable discomfort, with a certain thing?) Nevertheless, I found that my life would work better and things would be more peaceful around our house if I would just do what my daddy said to do. You know what? I didn't know it then, but my dad, the man from whom I inherited my "contrariness," taught me something important. To respect authority.

And that helped me learn to obey God. Somehow I understood the difference between the ambiguity of my daddy's parenting style and the wise, loving care of my heavenly Father. While there are times when a parent doesn't have a clear-cut reason for saying no, that's never so with our omniscient, sovereign God. He always knows what's best and forever has our best interests at heart. The thought of such love and compassion makes it easy to practice childlike obedience—even for a well-seasoned woman like me.

Another reason children are highly esteemed by God is their indifference to the things of this world. Their hearts are more centered on relationships, their

In the king-dom of God, simple truths are greatest; elemental ranks highest.

The Upside-Down Truth...

affections set upon the people they love instead of the things they possess. Jesus warned all of us not to be caught up in "the cares of this world" (Mark 4:19 NKJV). He knew that becoming an adult brings with it major concerns over the necessities of life, including money, family matters, health, and security. Even though the concerns are legitimate, if we worry and fret over them—or over the lack of them—they divert our attention away from God and can contaminate our closest relationships. As adults, we have to make a concentrated effort to keep from being swamped by the cares of this world.

Children are much more carefree. They live their lives in the present tense, just like we're supposed to do! It's easier for them because they don't have a past filled with regret, and their future stretches before them, promising all kinds of opportunity. Have you ever asked a child, "What do you want to be when you grow up?" Try it sometime and watch their eyes light up, their mind spinning as they think of all the possibilities. Unfortunately, most adults, at least those who have reached midlife, have become hardened by the experiences of life. They think they have already "become" all they will ever "be." Some have not realized their goals, others have lost hope, and some are settling into despair. Oh, to be more childlike in this regard!

$\mathcal{B}$e imitators of God, . . .
as dearly loved children.
Ephesians 5:1

One of my favorite photos is of our youngest grand-daughter, Abby. One evening when she and her sister Mary Catherine had come to our house for a sleepover, Abby ran to the trunk in our game room and pulled out a few things to play with. Before I even knew what was happening, she had donned a straw hat with a bright pink bow, a pair of sunglasses with multicolored frames, and a tiny pair of dressy high heels with feathers and sequins attached to the toe. A crocheted purse hung over her shoulder, and several strings of my old beads graced her neck. An extra dab of lip gloss added the perfect finishing touch to her very grown-up look.

She didn't make a single comment about her appearance when she strolled through the living room, plopped into a chair, and crossed her legs. With one leg swinging, she began to talk in grown-up tones. My hubby caught my eye and motioned for me to keep her talking while he ran for the camera. He knew this was a moment to record for the Malone family archives.

Why is that picture so precious to me? The most obvious reason is the simplest one. She looked cute as a button. But besides that, I love the picture because Abby had dressed in my stuff. A hat I'd once worn to a ladies' tea party. My old jewelry that I'd considered too gaudy to wear. A bag handmade by my mom. Abby looked like a miniature, out-of-date, but quite stylish version of her Grandma Gracie.

Isn't that interesting? Abby loves to play "grown-up," and I, now that I've reached the grandmother stage, find myself wanting to be young again. Abby likes to imitate me or one of my cohorts, and when I look at her and her group of playmates, I want to imitate them. And I'm not just talking about being young again physically.

Most children are light-years ahead of members of my generation when it comes to spiritual matters. I find myself wanting to imitate their childlike faith, their ability to simply trust God no matter what. I want their innocence, their simplicity of devotion. I desire their childlike sincerity along with their optimism and hope.

It is possible for me to become more like a child in these matters, but the change will not come by focusing on surface issues, donning a new hat, wearing high heels and pearls. I need to guard my heart; I can't allow myself to become hardened by the experiences of life. I can become like a child by simply trusting, quietly waiting on God.

I want to develop a childlike spirit in other ways as well. I want to go easy on myself when I goof up and learn to giggle over my blunders. I want more imagination, bigger dreams. I want to laugh and dance and play. I want to get enthused over the simple things of life, and I want to have more fun.

I don't know how you may be feeling right now, but I'm getting tired of growing older. I think most of us need to spend our remaining energy on growing young.

$\mathscr{R}$ight-Side Up

1. The apostle John often referred to his fellow believers as "little children." In 1 John 3:18, he instructed them about the matter of love. Perhaps they had become content with having surface relationships and he wanted them to go deeper with one another. What did he say? How are these words helpful for women today?

2. In Psalm 123:2, the psalmist uses analogies to help us see how we should look to God. How does this verse relate to having a childlike attitude? How does this verse encourage you?

3. Matthew 18:5–6 records Jesus's words about children and the inevitable "stumbling blocks" that would hinder or harm some of them. What is the warning given? How do these words impact you?

4. What does Matthew 18:10 teach about God's concern over the children of this world? Discuss the implications.

5. The message of John 14:27 is one much easier heeded by children than by adults. Why is it harder for adults to live by this admonition?

6. One of the characteristics of children that we admire most is their sincerity. Read Colossians 3:23–24. What do these verses say about living authentic, sincere lives?

7. First Corinthians 10:31 focuses on the phrase "whatever you do." Think about some of the "whatevers" in your life. What is it that you are doing for some other reason than for the "glory of God"?

~ 12 ~

In Dying, There Is Life

Living the ChristLife

For you died, and your life is now hidden with Christ in God.

Colossians 3:3

It is hard for most of us to think of ourselves as being "dead." But that's how God sees us. When we believe the truth about Jesus and accept him as our personal Lord, we are fundamentally changed. We are no longer "of this world" (John 8:23). Instead, we are so intimately related to Christ that God says we are "in him" (Eph. 1:4; Col. 2:10). As strange as that may seem to mortals like you and me, our union with Jesus has wonderful implications for us, beginning right now as we walk about on planet Earth and continuing throughout eternity.

For starters it means that when Jesus died for our sins, we died too. Being a Christian means we are dead to our old way of life. When Jesus was resurrected, we rose with him. Imagine that! We're not only dead but alive! Alive to God and to a new lifestyle where God is supreme. And there is more. Since Jesus is now seated in heaven at the right hand of God, we too are seated with him "in heavenly places," a sphere far above this world with its problems and pain.[1] The very thought of such a concept is more than a little mind-boggling.

When we come to Christ, all our sins are forgiven: past, present, and future—those we have already committed, those we are involved in right now, and those we haven't even thought about yet. What a blessed thought! But the spiritual truth goes even beyond forgiveness. We are *dead* to sin, so it has no power over us—no more than a virus would have over a lifeless corpse.[2] We are absolutely free from its control over our lives. How can that be? you may ask. If that's so, why do I still sin? Why do I sometimes make wrong choices? Why do I get involved in activities that feel good to my flesh and grieve the Spirit of God?

Maybe it's because we don't see ourselves as God sees us. Maybe we need to believe the truth about ourselves instead of the lies of our enemy. If God tells us we are dead, then we need to consider it so.[3] Tell it to yourself (out loud if you have to) and believe it. When Jesus suffered and died on the cross, he took our sins on himself. We are acceptable to God, not because we decided to be better people or because we promised to follow the rules, but because he took our sins away.[4] But that's just the half of it. He became sin for us so we could "become the righteousness of God in Him" (2 Cor. 5:21 NASB). He died for us; we died with him. What a great exchange! For us, anyway.

$\mathcal{H}$e died for us, so He could be formed in us.
Anonymous

Our problems with sin come when we don't exercise our faith. By not accepting the fact that we are a "new creation" (2 Cor. 5:17), dead to our old way of life, we can make what Jesus did on the cross of no effect, personally speaking, that is. The author of Hebrews claims we can actually be guilty of "crucifying the Son of God all over again and subjecting him to public disgrace" (Heb. 6:6). If the crucifixion of Christ has taken place once for all (and it has), what a *dis*-grace (literally) when we think of it as a simple historical fact, refusing to let it impact our daily lives.[5]

So how do we make the death of Christ a living reality? In part, by not only "considering" ourselves dead but by actually choosing to "die daily" (1 Cor. 15:31 NKJV) to certain activities and patterns that were a part of our old way of life.

Remember what happened following Jesus's triumphant entry into Jerusalem? The people had been dancing in the streets, waving palm branches, and extolling him as the King of the Jews. The disciples were caught up in the celebration too. Until Jesus called them aside and began talking about a most unlikely subject—death. "Unless a grain of wheat falls into the earth and dies, it remains alone; but if it dies, it bears much fruit" (John 12:24 NASB). Hmmm? Those early followers must have been as confused as we sometimes tend to be. They were ready for Jesus to be king. And they hadn't given up on the idea they would hold positions of honor in his kingdom. But Jesus wanted them to get it, once for all. His kingdom was not of this world! They would not be part of some notable earthly dynasty. It was time for the disciples to give up their human expectations, to die to their misguided plans and aspirations.

If you have ever had to let go of a dream, you know how the disciples must have felt at that moment. Perhaps your heart has been set on having a baby, but years have passed and there has been no conception. Maybe you had planned on graduating from college but an unexpected illness or trauma prevented you from getting your degree. Could be you thought your marriage would be a "till-death-do-us-part" kind of deal, but your husband left you for another woman. Maybe one of your children became an addict, or committed a criminal act. Perhaps you suffer from depression, feel discouraged, or have simply lost heart.

If any of those scenarios describe your life, or if one of a million other complexities have beset you, the same message Jesus spoke to his disciples is meant for you. I can almost hear him speaking out loud when I read from *The Message*: "Listen carefully: Unless a grain of wheat is buried in the ground, dead to the world, it is never any more than a grain of wheat. But if it is buried, it sprouts and reproduces itself many times over. In the same way, anyone who holds on to life just as it is destroys that life. But if you let it go, reckless in your love, you'll have it forever, real and eternal" (John 12:24–25 Message).

---

*W*hatever we do in this life is seed.
Thomas Manton

While it may be way outside your comfort zone, there comes a time to let go of some of the very things that have defined you in the past. Remember, as long as you hold on to the "seed," clutching it in your fist, it will never grow and multiply. Letting it go, dropping it into the warm soil of God's eternal purpose, gives it a chance to sprout into new life, to grow strong, and then to multiply. If you have a desire to multiply your ministry, to multiply the blessings of your family (or just multiply your family), then you will need to die—to your own agenda, to expecting things to happen a certain way, to being honored, to having a "successful" ministry or a perfect family. Letting go of our expectations is probably the greatest hurdle most Christian women must overcome.

When my friend Sara got married, she couldn't wait to have children.[6] "My greatest desire was to be a mom," she said. "I really wasn't interested in a career, didn't want to manage a business or have a huge ministry. I wanted to be a great parent." Within two years after her wedding, Sara gave birth to her first son, Kyle. Three years later she had a second, Mark, four years after that a beautiful daughter, Shelby. As the children grew up, Sara and her husband, Carl, enjoyed them. In fact, their lives revolved around the kids and their various activities.

They watched from the bleachers while their children played all kinds of sports from Little League, to volleyball, to high school football. In school, the kids made good grades and were well liked by their peers and teachers. Kyle was elected president of his high school's National Honor Society. All three children attended Sunday school, youth group, and summer camps. As teens, their lives seemed centered, focused on spiritual pursuits. Kyle played the guitar for youth choir. Mark enjoyed memorizing Scripture and sharing his faith. One summer he led backyard Bible studies in an economically challenged area and led several kids to accept Christ. He even spent several weeks following up on their decision, helping them become grounded in their newfound faith. Shelby served as youth intern her

first year of college. Sara couldn't help but be
proud of her brood, and rightfully so. They
were developing into fine young adults,
looking forward to a bright future.

But when the three moved away
from home and into college dorms
and student apartments, things
took a downward turn. Sara was
frightened by some of their choices.
To make matters worse, Carl separated himself from the family,
leaving critical decisions almost
completely in the hands and heart
of Sara. She tried to give counsel and
direction to her children while clinging to the hope that their struggles were
simply a part of growing up. She just knew
they'd find their footing and settle into a con-
sistent Christian lifestyle. Then she discovered they
were drinking and, to her dismay, doing drugs. Eventually
all three of Sara's precious children became addicted to different substances. One thing led to another, and today one child
is in prison on drug-related charges, another in rehab after
attempting suicide. The third is having marriage problems,
suffering panic attacks, and battling alcoholism.

How disheartening!

These circumstances have hurt Sara deeply. After the
prison thing, she thought she'd have a nervous breakdown.
She spent many a day in bed, the covers pulled up tightly
under her chin, rehearsing everything she had taught her
kids, second-guessing every parental decision. Did she force
her own beliefs on them, not giving them room to make
their own decisions? Was she too lenient? Or too strict? Was

> We are
> both dead
> and alive at
> the same time—
> dead to sin and
> alive to God.
>
> Warren Wiersbe

The Upside-Down Truth...

she blind to certain warning signs? Maybe she didn't pray enough, or in the right way. Maybe if she had prayed *really hard* . . . ! Sara became scared; her thoughts went round in circles. Occasionally she thought life just wasn't worth living. Then one day, in a spiritual breakthrough, Sara realized that she did indeed need to die—but not physically.

She made a long list of circumstances and problems she needed to lay on the altar, beginning with her expectations—to have a "perfect family," to enjoy a sterling reputation, to be recognized and respected, to be some sort of prototype of World's Best Mother. Basically, she needed to let her children make their own decisions and allow God to do his work in each life—in his own way, in his own time. She had to die to her desire to control their lives. I wish I could say that Sara's spiritual "death" was a once-for-all done deal. But the truth is, she has to die daily. Some days she is able to "let go and let God," but at other times she still finds herself trying to control or fix things.

Nevertheless, following her spiritual catharsis, things began to change. No, her children did not line up and head off to register at a nearby seminary. Nor did her husband suddenly reengage with the family. But the relationship between Sara and her children has become rock-solid, based on truth and openness. The kids communicate with each other too. The masks have been removed. Home is a place where everybody can talk about their problems, their addictive behaviors, their emotional struggles. All three children are even attending church, not as regularly as "Mama Sara" wants them to, but enough to give her hope. Sara knows she can't keep her kids from making mistakes, but no matter what they do, she's determined to be there for them, keeping the lines of communication open while "speaking the truth in love" (Eph. 4:15).

*H*ome should be a safe place to fall.
Dr. Phil

Death is a passage that's never easy to cross. But once Sara let go of her expectations, allowing the full head of "wheat" to fall on the ground, the kernels took root and produced a huge harvest. Sara's ministry multiplied like a crop of wild blackberries. Women know they can be real with her, and many of them talk to her with transparency about their own families. Sara's extended family members are learning valuable lessons too, including the fact that life is messy and complicated and that, almost universally, people stumble and fall. Sara knows it is always better to deal with whatever is true, rather than to deny or act as if problems don't exist. She prays that the younger members of the family will learn to deal with the people they love, including themselves, with authenticity and grace.

Giving up our expectations is just one way that women like you and me need to consider ourselves dead. My friend, a woman I'll call Carol, had to die to some of her old behavior patterns. She'd grown up with a domineering father and, as so often happens, married a man with similar personality traits. Fifteen years and two children into her marriage, Carol began to feel smothered and controlled. Yet, she couldn't seem to speak up for herself. But as she grew in her walk with Christ, she realized it was wrong to let herself be controlled by anybody—except the Holy Spirit.

It was time for her to die to being inactive and passive. It took time, but as Carol focused on who she was in Christ, she became more proactive and, in the process, much healthier, more in charge of her own destiny. She found the freedom to talk about her feelings, to take a stand on matters of conscience, and to take care of herself in ways she had never been able to do before. Today Carol's marriage is stronger than ever. Instead of depending on each other to get their needs met, both Carol and her husband have learned to seek God and to be interdependent with each other. They are more than happy; they are blessed because of the positive, albeit uncomfortable, changes Carol was willing to make.

What is it in your life that's causing you problems? Do you need to consider yourself dead toward certain attitudes and behaviors? Just in case you need a jump start to get you thinking, what about these:

- desiring to be understood
- finding favor with people
- thinking things will turn out a certain way
- arguing, making sure your position is heard
- showing favoritism, taking sides
- allowing the sin or problems of others to rob you of your peace and victory in Christ
- giving in to certain temptations
- fostering denominationalism
- holding on to tradition (if not biblically based)
- being burdened by legalism

In all our struggles, we need to remember that we are not only dead to sin but alive to God. Because of our identity with Christ, we possess within ourselves the life of the resurrection. The power of his Spirit resides in our hearts. And my union with him gives me all the strength and direction I need to live the Christian life in ways that please God. The truth is, there's no other way to live in victory and peace. Take a look at what Paul wrote to the Christians in Galatia:

> I tried keeping rules and working my head off to please God, and it didn't work. So I quit being a "law man" so that I could be God's man. Christ's life showed me how, and enabled me to do it. I identified myself completely with him. Indeed, I have been crucified with Christ. My ego is no longer central. It is no longer important that I appear righteous before you or have your good opinion, and I am no longer driven to impress God. Christ lives in me. The life you see me living is not "mine," but it is lived by faith in the Son of God, who loved me and gave himself for me. I am not going to go back on that.
>
> Is it not clear to you that to go back to that old rule-keeping, peer-pleasing religion would be an abandonment of everything personal and free in my relationship with God? I refuse to do that, to repudiate God's grace. If a living relationship with God could come by rule-keeping, then Christ died unnecessarily.
>
> Galatians 2:19–21 Message

Paul is talking here about his own life. He knew what it was like to live under the Mosaic law, so he speaks with authority to women like you and me. What he's saying is this: *I've tried living up to that standard, and it just didn't work for me. How's it working for you?* He's challenging us to follow his steps. *If you really believe the covenant that God made with Abraham, you will not allow yourself to settle for a life under the law.* Instead of all that rule keeping, Paul knew that he had been impaled to the cross and his life afterward was Christ living in him—plain and simple. Not Christ plus something, not Christ plus Sabbath keeping, not Christ plus circumcision. "Christ is my life!" he said. "And I live by faith in the one who loved me. To go back to the 'old rule-keeping, peer-pleasing religion' would mean turning my back on the grace of God, making his death completely unnecessary."

When we receive new life in Christ, we begin to walk in "newness of life" (Rom. 6:4 NKJV). And living life on a higher plane includes an active response on our part. For one thing, we're encouraged to "keep seeking the things above, where Christ is, seated at the right hand of God" (Col. 3:1 NASB). The verse is written in the present tense. That means we must seek-and-keep-on-seeking things that are part of the "above" zone. To clarify this even further, we're provided a checklist that includes certain attitudes and behaviors that we are to "put off" and others that we need to "put on." If you like spiritual truth to be clear and practical, take a look at these lists. Certain things we must be *dead toward*: immorality, impurity, passion, evil desire, and greed, which amounts to idolatry (Col. 3:5 NASB). A few things to *put aside*: anger, wrath, malice, slander, abusive speech, lies (vv. 8–9 NASB). A list of virtues to *put on*: a heart of compassion, kindness, humility, gentleness, patience, forbearance, forgiveness, and love (vv. 12–14 NASB). These spiritual values rooted in the heart of Christ are freely given to those who diligently seek them.

I think I know what your thoughts are after reading through these guidelines. *Well, that's the way I want to live, but how will I ever be able to measure up? The lists are clear, but how in the world can I accomplish such lofty goals?* Thankfully the same passage of Scripture gives us the solution to those troubling questions. First of all, success begins with our thoughts. It's all about our mind-set. "Set your mind on the things above, not on the things that are on earth" (Col. 3:2 NASB). This simply means that the choices we make, the way we direct our lives here on earth, should get their direction from Christ in heaven. Remember he is seated at the right hand of God, a fountain of bless-ing for all of us.[7]

We are dead to sin, alive to God, and seated in heaven with Christ, and amazing as it may seem, at the same time we are living in union with him here on earth. As the au-thor of Colossians put it, "your life is now hidden with Christ in God" (Col. 3:3).

The Upside-Down Truth...

I live to die,
I die to live;
the more I die,
the more I live.

When my kids were growing up, one of their favorite toys was an egg-shaped puzzle. It actually consisted of several eggs that nested together, each one fitting neatly inside another slightly bigger one. Each egg was painted to look like a child dressed in colorful garb with a pixie-like face. I remember a few times when the little egg puzzle, along with several other puzzles and blocks, would be scattered all over the floor of our kids' room. What a mess! Sometimes the task of cleaning up the room would com-pletely overwhelm my little boys. At times like that, what's a mom to do? I would sit on the floor beside my kids and help them sort the toys, coaching them as they put the puzzle pieces together again.

When it came to the egg puzzle, the first thing we had to do was locate the smallest pieces. We'd snap them together, then find the next larger parts and snap them around the smallest. The game would continue until all the egg-children were hidden inside the largest egg. I remember thinking at the time, *Isn't this exactly what our lives are like?* Jesus said,

The Upside-Down Truth...

"I am in My Father, and you in Me, and I in you" (John 14:20 NASB).

Since Christ lives in me, imagine one small egg labeled "Christ" tucked inside one labeled "me." Imagine the "me" egg nesting inside a bigger one marked "Christ." Then picture "Christ" fitting snugly inside the biggest egg, marked "God." What a safe place to hide.

We are living on earth, but we see it from heaven's point of view.

It seems to me that sin, in any of its insidious forms, would have a hard time getting through a shell of protection like that. But what happens if I play around outside my safe place? What if I forget who I am or "whose" I am? What if I allow myself to be tossed around carelessly and my life becomes fragmented and scattered? Maybe then we could use a little help to pick up the pieces. A good place to begin would be reminding each other: *Christ lives in me. I am alive in him.*

_Right-Side Up

1. Put it in your own words: what does it mean to die to sin?

2. This chapter lists several things women need to consider themselves dead toward. Think about your own life. What are some things you need to let go of?

3. Read Philippians 3:10–11. What are the four desires of the apostle Paul? Meditate on these desires of Paul and discuss your thoughts. Does Paul express the desires of your heart?

4. What are some of the things you want to become "alive to" as you seek the things above?

5. Read John 8:31–32. What sets us free from our old way of life?

6. What does Colossians 2:12–14 teach about our union with Christ in his death, burial, and resurrection?

7. Read the following verses. Discuss ways they help us "walk in newness of life."
   - Romans 13:14
   - Galatians 5:16
   - 2 Corinthians 4:10
   - Ephesians 1:3

8. If we learn to be dead to sin and alive to God, and if we are seated in the heavenlies, what will our lives look like here on earth? See Matthew 5:13–14.

Afterword

One morning, before I booted up my computer to write the final pages of this book, I paused to read from Oswald Chambers's classic devotional work *My Utmost for His Highest*. It's something I have done every day this year. But on this occasion, as I began to read, I found myself wondering how his words penned in the early 1900s could have been so perfect for me on this cloudy December day some one hundred years later. Seems to me this man was so in tune with God, his writing is still able to reach out and touch women like you and me, right where we live, today. That said, I'm going to let you read part of what Chambers wrote:

> If you cannot express yourself well on each of your beliefs, work and study until you can. If you don't, other people may miss out on the blessings that come from knowing the truth. Strive to re-express a truth of God to yourself clearly and understandably, and God will use that same explanation when you share it with someone else. But you must be willing to go through God's winepress where the grapes are crushed. You must struggle, experiment, and rehearse your words to express God's truth clearly. Then the time

will come when that very expression will become God's wine of strength to someone else. . . .

Always make it a practice to stir your own mind thoroughly to think through what you have easily believed. Your position is not really yours until you make it yours through suffering and study. The author or speaker from whom you learn the most is not the one who teaches you something you didn't know before, but the one who helps you take a truth with which you have quietly struggled, give it expression, and speak it clearly and boldly.[1]

Why did those words help me so much on that one particular day? Because I was struggling. Trying to make sense of a reality I'd heard all my life, but for some reason couldn't put into words. How can a person be dead, but alive? How can I be troubled with the happenings of life when I am seated in the heavenlies? The mental aerobics exercising my brain on this day were not much different from those of other days, except that I was tired. And what a difference that makes!

Every chapter I've written has literally turned me upside down, inside out, and right-side up. And all the while life has gone on happening—and not always smoothly. Before I could write about spiritual death for example, I had to die to a gazillion different circumstances and emotions. And God is not finished with me yet! But how exciting to know that he is faithful—not only helping me let go (sometimes prying my fingers off something I'm holding too tightly), but also lifting me up again and showing me how to live in the power of his resurrection.

So what about you? Did Oswald Chambers write to you too? I hope so! For if you simply read what I have written and do not make it your own, the truths will quickly vanish from your thoughts, making no real difference in your life.

How do you make the truth your own? What does it mean to "stir your own mind"? What's the best way to "thoroughly think through what you have easily believed"? Thankfully, the apostle Paul has told us exactly what to do. "Let the word of Christ richly dwell within you, with all wisdom teaching and admonishing one another with psalms and hymns and spiritual songs, singing with thankfulness in your hearts to God" (Col. 3:16 NASB).

Now, you have known me long enough to know that I can never leave you with a verse without trying to explain what it says. So here goes (briefly of course!). First of all, remember it is "the word of Christ" that's important. Not the words of the press, not whatever is politically correct, not the words of Gracie or even those of Chambers, but the Word of Christ.

We're to let his Word "richly dwell" in us. "Dwell" means much more than taking a casual glance into Scripture. It means finding time every day to dig deeply, giving truth an opportunity to settle down and make its home in your heart. The truth will dwell in us "richly" when we search out the true meaning of the original words, when we compare different texts, when we meditate and pray. (Why not splurge on a new concordance? I love the *Strong's* that includes the best of *Vine's Dictionary*.) The verse also promises the wisdom we need to teach and "admonish" or counsel one another. Most importantly, that kind of Bible study will honor God. We'll find ourselves celebrating with "psalms and hymns and spiritual songs," our hearts filled to overflowing with thankfulness.

If we would know the truth, there's no doubt we must work hard. And yes, there will be times we are squeezed in "God's winepress." I don't suppose you'd find a single one of us pushing to the front of the line at the grape-crushing machine, but in the process we'll find truth that will make a major difference in the lives of our family and friends! In addition, we get to become "God's wine," a woman who's full of the effervescent joy of Jesus, willing to spill over into a world of hurt, bringing blessing and peace and wisdom. Why, it's enough to make this straitlaced, Baptist-bred woman want to jump up and down for joy.

My prayer is that you will join me in the pursuit and in the celebration that's bound to follow.

> For you will go out with joy
> And be led forth with peace;
> The mountains and the hills will break forth into
>   shouts of joy before you,
> And all the trees of the field will clap their hands.

Isaiah 55:12 NASB

Notes

Chapter 1 A New Way of Living

1. "Island Tribes Begin to Emerge after Tsunami," NPR.org, http://www.npr
.org/templates/story/story.php?storyId=4270615.

Chapter 2 The Way Up Is Down

1. See Daniel 4:27 NASB

2. See Philippians 1:6

3. See Galatians 6:3

4. Brennan Manning, *Reflections for Ragamuffins* (New York: HarperCollins,
1998), 197.

5. See Proverbs 4:23; Proverbs 23:7 KJV; Galatians 6:3–4

6. Stephen Arterburn, *More Jesus, Less Religion* (Colorado Springs: Waterbrook,
2000), 111.

Chapter 3 Whoever Is Last Will Be First

1. See John 13:1–17; 21:9–14

2. See Mark 9:34

3. See Matthew 20:24

4. See 2 Timothy 2:12; Revelation 5:10

5. See Ephesians 2:4–6

6. See Matthew 5:1–12

7. Oswald Chambers, *My Utmost for His Highest, An Updated Version in Today's
English*, ed. James Reimann (Cedar Rapids, IA: Parson's Technology, 1998),
August 21.

8. See Isaiah 55:11

Chapter 4 In Giving We Receive

1. See Matthew 10:8

2. See Luke 6:27–29

3. See Luke 6:37

4. See John 14:31
5. See Matthew 5:42
6. See Colossians 3:15
7. Larry Burkett, *Your Finances in Changing Times*, rev. ed. (Chicago: Moody Press, 1993), 105.
8. See Matthew 27:55–56

Chapter 5 When the Going Gets Tough, the Tough . . . Rest

1. See Genesis 1
2. See Genesis 2:2–3 NASB
3. See Job 38:4–7
4. See Genesis 7:1
5. Genesis 7:9: "Pairs of . . . animals . . . came to Noah and entered the ark."
6. Chambers, *My Utmost for His Highest*, June 11.
7. AARP, "Grandparenting" 2004, www.aarp.org/confacts/grandparents/pdf/G_Census_Table_1.pdf.
8. See John 6:63
9. See Hebrews 4:13
10. See Mark 1:14–34 NASB
11. See Mark 1:31

Chapter 6 Definitely Flawed, Yet Deeply Loved

1. www.harmonize.com/probe/aids/misc/Songtitles.htm
2. Eugene Peterson, "Introduction: 1, 2, & 3 John," *The Message* (Colorado Springs: NavPress, 1993), 500.
3. Song of Solomon 1:2
4. See John 4:9 NASB
5. See John 12:3–7
6. See Song of Solomon 5:16 KJV
7. See Hebrews 4:15
8. See 1 John 4:9–10
9. See John 4:39b
10. See Colossians 2:10 NASB; 2 Corinthians 5:21; Romans 6:18, 22; Galatians 5:1

Chapter 7 Discovering Strength in Weakness

1. See Romans 8:28
2. See 1 Corinthians 10:13 NASB
3. Mrs. Charles Cowman, *Streams in the Desert* (Los Angeles: Cowman Publications, Inc., 1925), 109, emphasis in original.

Chapter 8 Finding Joy in Trials

1. See 2 Corinthians 12:2–4
2. T. W. Hunt and Melana Hunt Monroe, *From Heaven's View* (Nashville: Broadman & Holman, 2002), 73–74.
3. Ibid.

4. See Revelation 21:18
5. See Revelation 21:19–20
6. See Hebrews 12:2
7. See 1 Peter 1:6; Genesis 37:3

Chapter 9 Seeing Light in the Darkness

1. Found in Hebrews 11
2. See Romans 10:17
3. See Romans 1:17
4. See Galatians 3:11
5. See Hebrews 10:38
6. Kay Arthur, *Lord, Where Are You When Bad Things Happen?* (Sisters, OR: Multnomah, 1992), 134.

Chapter 10 Working Out What God Works In

1. See Philippians 1:1
2. Warren Wiersbe, *Be Joyful* (Whitby, Ontario: Victor Books, 1974), 70.
3. Cynthia Spell Humbert, *Deceived by Shame, Desired by God* (Colorado Springs: NavPress, 2001).
4. See Hosea 6:3 KJV
5. See Acts 9:3–6
6. See Acts 8:3; Galatians 1:13
7. See Acts 9:1–2
8. See James 2:17, 20
9. See 1 Corinthians 6:19–20 NASB
10. See Philippians 1:6
11. See 2 Peter 3:17–18; Romans 8:28
12. See 1 Peter 2:2

Chapter 11 Maturing into Childhood

1. See Romans 3:22–24
2. Chambers, *My Utmost for His Highest*, September 14.
3. Ibid.

Chapter 12 In Dying, There Is Life

1. See Ephesians 2:6
2. See Romans 6:2
3. See Romans 6:11
4. See 1 John 3:5
5. See Galatians 2:21
6. The names for members of this family are pseudonyms.
7. See 1 Peter 3:22

Afterword

1. Chambers, *My Utmost for His Highest*, December 15.

Gracie Malone is a Precept Bible Study leader and mentor to women. *LifeOvers* is her life message—the book she's always wanted to write. She is the author or coauthor of several books, including *Kisses of Sunshine for Grandmas*, *Off My Rocker*, and *Still Making Waves*, and a contributor to magazines like *Discipleship Journal* and *Christian Parenting Today*.

A much-loved inspirational speaker at women's conferences and retreats, Gracie brings God's truths to life through her unique style of humor, heart-warming anecdotes, and thought-provoking insights. Her transparent and down-to-earth stories often include her family: one patient husband, three adult sons, and six amazing grandkids. Becoming a grandmother hasn't slowed her down: "You won't find me sitting on the porch, knitting those little hot-pad thingies!"

Gracie and her husband, Joe, make their home in Grapevine, Texas. Visit Gracie's website at www.graciemalone .com.